The Very Simple
Law of Attraction

The Very Simple Law of Attraction

An Introduction to
Diamond Feng Shui

by Marie Diamond

MEDIA

Published 2019 by Gildan Media LLC
aka G&D Media
www.GandDmedia.com

THE VERY SIMPLE LAW OF ATTRACTION. Copyright © 2007, 2019 by Marie Diamond. All rights reserved.

Published by Arrangement with Burman Books

Interior design by Meghan Day Healey of Story Horse, LLC

Library of Congress Cataloging-in-Publication Data is available upon request

ISBN: 978-1-7225-0020-7

10 9 8 7 6 5 4 3 2 1

Dedication

With gratitude to all past and present teachers
and mentors on my path.

With gratitude to all my students and clients
on my journey.

With gratitude to my family and friends
for their patience and support.

Contents

Acknowledgments

My first acknowledgment is to the Universe for being what it is—an unlimited source of energy, information, love, and inspiration for what I bring to the world.

My second acknowledgment is to my father, Prudent. He passed away when I was twenty-five years old. He believed in me and told me that I would make a difference in the world. Depending on his mood he wanted me to be a Catholic nun or a judge. He didn't know the word Feng Shui Master: I work with the laws of Universe/God. It just has another name dad.

My third acknowledgment is to my mother, Marguerite. At seventy-five years of age she started using my information about the law of attraction in her home. I believe that her belief is a part of her great health today and her wonderful spirit. Thank you mama, for your amazing support all these years, even if you didn't understand what I was doing, you always went along.

My fourth acknowledgment is to my husband Jean Marie and my children Anthony, Andres, and Enya for allowing me to change our homes over and over again. With their persistence and my persistence they were the ideal base for studying Feng Shui and trying out my new ideas and colors. Thank you for allowing me to express myself so I could share my gifts with the world.

My last acknowledgment is to my source. Thank you for being so generous in providing the right information and connections at the right time and the right place.

Preface

When Sanjay Burman came to me with the idea to collaborate and create a TV show and a book, I fell in love with the idea. Writing this book has deepened my own knowledge of how the law of attraction and Feng Shui work together. It helped me to analyze the stories of my clients, their testimonials, and improve my knowledge all over again.

This book will help you to understand how your environment is a reflection of who you are and what you have been attracting and receiving in your life, and perhaps, lacking.

Writing *The Very Simple Law of Attraction* made me look again at my own home and office; what I have been attracting and receiving in my life. I was already very successful and happy, but while writing and implementing the information I am sharing here I have grown tremendously and my revenues have doubled since I started this book. New exciting projects keep pouring in. So, I can tell you that I knew it worked, but refocusing brought me to another level of attraction. I definitely received more recognition and power, more clarity, and more magnificence in my life.

My wish for you is that this book makes you aware of the greatness that your environment can bring you when you implement the law of attraction in your own home and office.

Wishing you double happiness—inside out and outside in.

Marie Diamond

www.theverysimplelawofattraction.com

www.mariediamond.com

Introduction

~~~~~~

Life is really quite simple—so are the laws of the Universe/ God.

A law is a principle that works each time for each person in all conditions.

It is a principle that is beyond culture, color, country, gender, and age. It works the same for the rich or for the poor, for the famous and for everyday people.

It is a principle that is beyond time: it has worked in every part of history, it works now, and it will work in the future. The caveman used it, the Greek philosopher, the people in the Middle Ages, today's modern woman and man; they perhaps didn't know they practiced this principle but they did then, and they do now.

It is a principle that is beyond space: it works in every home wherever you live; in every office wherever you work; it works in the rainforest and it works in Los Angeles.

The very simple law of attraction is the very simple principle that you are a human being living in a certain time and in a certain space and that your alignment through thoughts, feelings, and actions will bring exactly to you what you have aligned yourself with.

The Universe/God does not differentiate. The same reaction will be given to everyone, every time and in every place. You receive back what you ask for. The Universe/God loves you unconditionally and returns your messages to Him/Her/It with excellent service. It is the greatest customer service out there: you receive your order at the right time in the right place with the Universal delivery system. You just don't know when that right time is or where the right place is, and you don't know how it is going to be delivered; something greater than our understanding is working on this Universal fulfillment.

So why do we not receive exactly what we ask for?

You are getting back what you've asked for. But you may not be conscious about what it is that you have actually asked for. It is possible that you are continually contradicting yourself and screwing up the Universal delivery system. Have you ever picked the petals off a flower? I love him, I don't love him, I'll marry him, and I won't marry him. You are the one ordering both ways.

How does that happen?

The issue is that you need to send the right messages out through your human email service.

You have two kinds of messages you send to the Universe/God:

The first one is the conscious message: you are asking consciously and sending out a message by praying, meditating, doing affirmations, talking to God, the Universe, angels or masters. You ask towards a higher awareness because you feel that the answers will be given to you in a form of inspiration: through people, in a dream, by intuition, or simply by God speaking to you. There are many forms of direct messaging to the Universe/God and they are all good.

The second form of message you send out is what you do without really focusing consciously. By living your daily life and having your thoughts, feelings, and actions just unfold. In your talking, swearing, telling stories, feeling your emotions, reacting to other people in a positive or a negative way, watching television, listening to music; you are sending out a message that what you align yourself with is actually what you wish for more of in the future.

The alignment you create between the Universe/God and your environment is in the unconscious part of the messages that you send.

Your home or office is the first expression of your creation; the Universe within you and the reflection of your creation to the outside world.

Let's put it very simply; your home is the bridge between what you create with your thoughts, feelings and actions, and the world outside of you. It is the first layer of the world outside of you.

What you surround yourself with is constantly giving unconscious messages to the Universe—and not occasionally, but constantly. It is communicating with the Universe twenty-four hours a day, three-hundred and sixty-five days a year.

In the hit movie *The Secret*, I talk about a man that surrounded himself with seven images of women that did not appear to be interested in him. In his home he aligned himself with a constant unconscious message to the Universe that he did not want women to look at him. How could he then attract women to his home that would love him?

What was not shown in the movie was that this man had put these seven images in seven different rooms in his home. Each image in each room faced the same compass direction; his personal relationship direction.

Every person needs to align his conscious messages with his unconscious messages.

This man wanted romance but his unconscious messages, reflected in the images that he had around him in his home, contradicted that. What did the Universe hear the most? Was it the few times he prayed for a woman to love him or the twenty-four hour a day message of the seven images placed in the perfect angle to the Universe?

The very simple law of attraction will reveal to you how to exactly align your conscious requests with your environment so that you will have a twenty-four hour constant connection service to the Universe.

I have known the law of attraction since I was seven years old and I have learned how much easier it is to receive my requests when I have confirmed them by placing them in the right place. The Universal delivery system can then receive them constantly and without effort.

Diamond Feng Shui teaches you how you can align your inner wishes with your environment; how you can exactly place your requests so the Universe can receive them immediately and constantly.

The Three Levels of the Law of Attraction

By studying Feng Shui I came to understand that there are three levels of the law of attraction.

The first level is one that operates in the process of attraction when we are born. Your parents attracted you in, consciously or unconsciously, by their thoughts, feelings or actions; they received you in their life. You as a soul attracted your parents, your country, and your life conditions.

Some would call this your destiny, your faith or karma. The ones who believe in previous life experiences would say you attracted this in because of your thoughts, feelings, and actions from a previous life.

The Feng Shui Masters expressed that this level of the law of attraction accounts for one third of your good luck. So, your destiny has only a one third influence on your life.

Can we change this part of the law of attraction?

At first glance not really, because where you are born and the parents you have will keep influencing you in a certain way. The talents you are born with will be there for you to use. Elders in many religious or spiritual forms of expression tell us that we can change our destiny; that is not what this book is about, but let's hope we are successful in doing so.

The second level of the law of attraction is called human luck. It is the part that most self-help authors and speakers talk about. Most people use this luck unconsciously and create a reality around them in the exact way they have focused their thoughts, feelings, and actions. More than eighty percent of the global population is still asleep. They are not even aware that they have created exactly what they have been focusing on; they repeat the same patterns over and over again.

Once someone hits rock bottom in their misery, they then start asking questions: Why is this happening to me? Whose fault is this that I feel so bad, that all this bad luck happens to me, that I attracted this abusive partner, or that I get laid off; the possibilities are endless. Of course when you are not consciously awake you try to blame it first on everything outside of you: your wife, your husband, your children, your boss, your mother, and finally if you can't find anybody else—God.

They remain attracting in exactly what they have been focusing on because blame doubles the effect: more abuse, more bad luck, more lack of money.

Then when the light bulb finally goes on or the egg of misery cracks open—hallelujah—they see that perhaps they created this themselves. Blaming someone else didn't change anything, but what if I start to look at myself?

The awakening process starts happening: a book, a film, some advice, a church sermon, an AA meeting. You may hear it said that: You are the creator of your own life. God is in you. You are responsible for your own addiction. You are the divine within.

Let's be honest, in the beginning you get it but you turn it away immediately thinking that it is too simple or too hard. Even if you get it, it is still hard for many people to start living with this new wisdom.

According to the Feng Shui Masters, this level of the law of attraction is also one third of your good luck. You can change this but even then you have not changed all the odds.

I am sure you have been to many workshops and read many books that give you great tools to use to change this third of your luck around. You have an "aha" moment, you understand your problem. You promise to change but before you know it life overtakes your desire for change and your "aha" moment is not followed up. Many people have asked me why that happens.

While researching over the years I found the answers. It is not because something changes in your thoughts, feelings, and actions that you integrate that change in your life. You need to understand that what is around you also influences you and if your environment is not supporting your inner changes, the changed attitude is not rooted in your current reality.

That is where earth luck, the third level of the law of attraction, comes in. Around your physical body, you also have aura fields where your thoughts and feelings are reflected. You also have another layer where your life is reflected. It is the space around you where you live, sleep, and work. It is the place where you act upon your thoughts and feelings. It is the bridge between your inner self and the outer world.

You want the Universe to bring forward your requests, but these gifts need to show up in the outside world around you. If you start to change your outside world to reflect those changes that you want to happen, the Universe starts to act faster.

Someone told me once, "fake it till you make it". If you start showing the Universe what you want by faking it in your own home then the results will arrive faster than before.

I once wished that one day I could meet Leonardo Di Caprio. So, I faked it by hanging his picture, taken from the internet, on my vision board. Each time I walked in to the room my vision board was in I spoke to his picture as if I was meeting him in reality. "Hi," I said, "how are you doing?" Then I let the Universe do its magic.

I got a call from New York to visit a client that I had not met before I put the picture up. The next day as I was leaving her apartment for another appointment she told me that the penthouse of her apartment building was owned by the, at that time, girlfriend of Leonardo. I had not told her of my request to the Universe; she spontaneously started talking about him.

It was raining as I left the building and waved for a taxi. A gentleman in a baseball cap stopped a taxi, opened the door and offered me his cab: It was Leonardo Di Caprio.

In this book, *The Very Simple Law of Attraction*, I will show you in twenty-four chapters how to attract and receive what you want from the Universe by placing the right images around you and using the right colors.

When I walk in a home or office, I see what you have already attracted. You reflect exactly what you wish for, you just don't know it. If I can see from what I see around you and know it from what your life looks like, don't you think that the Universe has understood your message too and created for you exactly what you put outside of your-self?

The Universe just thinks that this is exactly what you wish to happen and gives in perfect order what you wish for. I can tell you that this part of the law of attraction is the easiest to change. Changing your images, decluttering, or painting is something you can do immediately. The best part about this change is that you can ask others to help you, or even do it for you, but once it is done, the impact is the same.

When you start faking something else, the Universe will read exactly what your wish is and it will make it happen. When, I don't know. How, I don't know; that is up to the Universe to create.

I remember I saw the movie *Funny Girl* with Barbra Streisand when I was a young girl. Using what I knew already about Feng Shui, I put a picture out in my success area with this request: I wish I could hear her sing in my life in a concert. At that time there was no way that

I could ever imagine or know that one day, while I was already living in Los Angeles, my husband would buy me, as a forty-fourth birthday gift, tickets for the last concert of her rare concert tours.

Just thirty meters from me, Barbra Streisand sang all the songs that I love so much and experiencing that helped me through a difficult time in my life. I just cried the whole concert, knowing that the Universe had given exactly what I asked for as a young woman. It had just taken time for the pieces to come together. Barbra rarely tours in Europe and hadn't toured since I had lived in the United States. But from the first moment my wish could be true, it happened. My husband didn't know that wish of mine, he was inspired by the Universe to buy this ticket after listening to the radio one morning. I know that if I hadn't hung her picture in my bedroom for a while, almost two years, and made my request, it would not have happened.

Can you change this part of the law of attraction?

You can and it is easy. As Donald Trump, a big fan of Feng Shui, once said to my Grand Master, "If by changing my desk, I can make more millions, why not?"

The Very Simple Law of Attraction and Diamond Feng Shui

When Feng Shui started coming into my life, I knew I had found a magical wand. It was the missing link to creating my wishes in my life quickly and effortlessly. Diamond Feng Shui is my way of combining traditional classical

Feng Shui with quantum physics. Helping you change your thoughts, feelings, and actions by first changing the outside. It is an easier way to start the process of change and your thoughts, feelings, and actions will start to change because your unconscious focus will be different. Your inspiration and aspirations will start shifting. In the Diamond Feng Shui home study course that I created with Learning Strategies Inc., we did tests that showed that your brainwaves change when your environment is changed.

When a person was in a place with clutter, the encephalogram immediately showed indication of beta brainwaves which create a lack of inspiration and even depressive moods. When the same person was placed in a Diamond Feng Shui office they immediately showed alpha brainwaves which create inspiration and optimistic moods.

So what you see around you immediately influences brainwaves. As you are the Universe, you also are receiving other messages and you accordingly create a different reality.

In this book, I will give you the twenty-four different aspects of a diamond to focus on and to use to make the reality you want.

Twelve of the aspects of the diamond are male and you send the message out.

Twelve of the aspects of the diamond are female and you receive the message in.

I give you a personal Marie Diamond story for each subject, tips on how to create another reality by using your home or office, a special color to use to bring in even more of this new reality you wish to create, and some special affirmations.

Good luck.

Remember you are the creator of your Universe and your home and office is part of your Universe.

Note: Your personal best direction is based on your date of birth. To find out your personal best direction, visit www.theverysimplelawofattraction.com.

Chapter 1

Do You Attract Power?

When I was twenty-six years old I got a new job as a lawyer in an international publishing company. I had heard that every one before me had only lasted for about six months in this job. I wondered why as the job was fun and inspiring. I soon found out. I was sitting with my back towards the rest of the team. They indeed talked behind my back. I was sitting with my back to the entrance of the office and on top of this, with my back towards the desk of my manager. She put everything I suggested to her for articles in the garbage bin or gave it to one of my colleagues; no support there at all, in fact the exact opposite.

I had started to understand why people change so I asked if I could turn my desk around to see the team but my request was denied. So I placed a little mirror next to me so that I could see what was going on with the team and with my manager. She started to like my ideas and to let me write them. I also got more and more support from some of the team. There was one person that I couldn't see from my mirror and that person continued to ignore me After six months I was transferred and in the new office I insisted that I be able to position my desk the way I wanted. I positioned myself as a queen: I could see the door and I had a very high backed chair.

In the following year I was promoted twice and earned double what I had made when I started with the company. I know I couldn't have attracted this new job without this little mirror.

The First Step
Analyze Your Life: Do You Feel in Power?

Before you start creating change in your life, it is good to stand still and ask yourself some questions.

I will help you with this analysis. When I enter people's homes and lives, I ask them questions.

In the busy life you live you need to stop for five minutes and ask yourself, do I have a problem? Only when you are aware you have a situation to change, can you really take the steps and start changing.

If you feel that any of your answers to the following questions is not a complete yes, than it will be good to check out the next steps I give you to improve the power in and around you.

Questions

- Do you feel safe in your life and your environment?
- Do you feel supported by your boss or manager?
- Do you feel supported in your life by your family and loved ones?
- Do you feel confident that you will attain your goals?
- Do you feel that you live to your full potential?
- Are you at the place in your life where you wish to be?
- Are you in a powerful position in your career?
- Do you receive praise for your talents and accomplishments?

The Second Step

Analyze Your Home: Do You Attract Power in Your Home or Office?

As I explained already, your home is the unconscious expression from within yourself. When I enter a home or office I always look for signs to see if the people there feel powerful.

As you are the Universe you need to be in power in your life. People that are not in power are not attracting what they really desire. They will stay in a poverty consciousness; they will feel vulnerable and weak. They will feel like victims of their reality instead of being the masters of their lives.

The European kings and queens, the emperors of China were looking to have a long and powerful government; they wanted to be the masters of their countries. Your life is like a country. You wish to be the master of yourself and make your dreams come true.

This checklist will show you what to look for that will indicate whether you are the master in your universe or a victim of your reality.

Sitting as a Master in Your Home or Office
Do you see the gifts of the Universe come to you or do you sit with your back to them?

At your office, your desk, or any space you work in, make sure you sit in such a way that you can see the incoming energy. The Universe comes through the door and not through the windows. The Universe walks in when you walk in. People that walk are the Universe.

Obvious Signs That You Are the Master of Your Universe
When you enter your home you see that:
- You are facing the door or the hallway when watching TV.
- You are facing the entrance of your home office.
- You are facing the entrance of the area that you work out or exercise in.
- You are facing the door or entrance of your dining room when eating.
- You can see someone enter the bedroom when you are sleeping there. If not, you have hung a little mirror so you can see the door when you wake up.

Extra Tip
- Even if you go to dinner at a restaurant or if you are in a meeting or in a conference room, never sit with your back to the entrance. From now on you wish always to be the master of your own life.

Support From the Universe Around You

When you look at the kings and queens and emperors, they were always supported at their back by the Universe. The Universe is not only God or an expression of the divine energy; it is also expressed through people in power that are supporting you.

A king or queen will all ways sit on a throne that supports their back and neck. Their arms are resting on the chair. Don't you wish to have the same support?

Obvious Signs That You Allow the Support of the Universe in Your Life

When you enter your home you see that:

☙ You are sitting on a chair with a high back.

☙ You are not sitting on a chair with slats.

☙ You are not sitting on an old chair that is almost falling apart.

☙ You are not sitting on an open bench or on the ground to watch TV.

☙ You are sitting on a couch with back support.

☙ You are sleeping in a bed with a headboard and not on a mattress on the floor.

☙ You are not sleeping in a bed made with metal or wooden slats.

Solutions

☙ Buy a high-backed chair and place it behind your desk; especially if you are still sitting with your back to the door.

☙ Cover the back of your chair with fabric or place a pillow between you and the back of the chair.

☞ Remove the old chair and find a newer one to sit on.

☞ Place pillows on the bench.

☞ Place a headboard at the end of your bed to support your head or start by placing pillows between your head and the wall.

☞ Place your mattress on another mattress or on bricks or anything you can find to use that brings it about thirty centimeters or one foot up from the floor.

☞ Cover metal or wooden slats with fabric or place pillows up against the slats.

☞ If you can't do anything like this, make sure you place symbolic support behind you.

Extra Tips

☞ Remove any chair that needs repair.

☞ You can also place a rock, a Buddha statue, or an image of an angel behind your home and opposite the front door.

☞ Place an image of a mountain behind you for support.

☞ Place a large round-leaved plant behind you for support.

Create a Powerful Home

The images/statues that are hung in your home represent you. The more powerful the images/statues are the more you will attract being treated as a powerful person.

Depending on what you wish to accomplish and in what area you wish to be powerful, your imageries will be different. If you wish to be a powerful scientist then make sure you hang an image of Einstein or Newton in your living or workspace. If you wish to be an author that is still read after five hundred years, try Shakespeare. For those in real estate who wish to become billionaires, an image of Donald Trump could be ideal. Make sure that you resonate personally with the images. If you don't like the person, don't use the image; this person needs to feel good to you.

What Are Powerful Images?

- Images of successful people in your profession.
- Images of people who have won awards connected with your goal.
- Images of your idols and heroes, past and present.
- Images of famous people.
- Images of mountains.
- Images of your masters, CEO, or managers.
- Images of certificates.
- Images of Buddha, Jesus, angels.
- Statues of awards like Oscars with your name on it.
- Front covers of books and magazines with your image on them.
- Images of your products in a golden frame.
- Images of royal or imperial figures.
- Images of people you admire.
- Images of your logos, advertising or marketing materials and articles.
- A Vision Board.
- Your goals.

Where Should You Hang Your Powerful Images?

☞ Make sure you have powerful images at the entrance to your business.

☞ Place them in the south area of your office.

☞ Behind your chair so you feel supported by powerful people.

☞ Facing where you sit so you can focus on successful people.

☞ You can also hang images in your personal best direction in your living, family room, bedroom and your office.

☞ Place the Power Affirmations given to you by Marie Diamond on an index card and also place it in your personal power direction.

Extra Tips

☞ Remove clutter from the entrance.

☞ Remove any garbage bins or laundry baskets from your personal power direction.

☞ Remove all images in your home that do not convey power or success.

The Third Step
The Color of Power—Royal Blue

The Universe responds to symbols and images but also to colors. Royal Blue is the color of power and using it will help you to attract a position of power in your life and career.

The name Royal Blue already tells you—you are royalty. The origin of the word "royal" comes from the French "roial"—the king of all. You are the king or queen of everything in your life.

How can you use this color?

☙ Wear this color as an accessory if you feel it will support you in a powerful way.

☙ Place a royal blue item in the north area of your bedroom, office or living room to attract more power to your life.

Conclusion

Take every step that you can to bring more power into your life. Even small steps help. The small mirror in my personal story created a shift of power.

It took me a while to get the change to happen, but change will occur.

If you don't have powerful images already, start attracting them in your life and you will start receiving gifts that are powerful to hang. Once you allow yourself to be open to being a master in your own life you will be treated as one.

POWER AFFIRMATIONS

I open myself to experience the power
that I have.

I create the place around me that will help
me to experience this power in me.

I allow myself to be a king or a queen in my life,
making powerful decisions and reaching
my full potential.

Chapter 2

~~~~~~

Do You Attract Empowerment?

As I became well-known as a self-help teacher and Feng Shui expert in my home country of Belgium, I began to feel that I was getting closer to fulfilling my dream of creating a better world for millions of people by giving them the tools to transform themselves by using meditations and changing their environment.

It was then that I attracted in my life a very powerful business person as a client. I started really looking up to him; I was flattered that he liked me and honored my professional advice. But he told me many times, "Marie you are a little shrimp and you will never become a lobster." Let's be honest, that is not very empowering. But because he said this, I felt that I would prove he was wrong.

What he didn't know is that my rising sign in western astrology is Cancer, making me a lobster figuratively speaking. I started to understand that his method to keep me around him and serve his interests was to make me feel small. If he had given me compliments and I felt stronger, perhaps he would have lost me.

I started making changes in my life using the right attitude; I was ready to manifest my inner power. Now, he is still a powerful but older business person in Belgium and I have manifested my goals more than ever. Sometimes empowerment is in being courageous and believing in yourself even if powerful people don't believe in you or use you for their own interests.

He was afraid to lose me and he lost me anyway. Empowering others to grow, you perhaps will lose them but they will remain your friend and start collaborating with you.

The First Step

Analyze Your Life: Are You Feeling Empowered?

Empowerment means that you move forward with confidence in your life.

When you have opened yourself to the power of the Universe you will feel empowered. Empowering is about radiating the power in yourself AND sharing with others the messages that changed your life.

Empowerment is how you manifest your power in your life and how others feel your ease and confidence in using the law of attraction.

Questions

- Do you feel courageous in your life?
- Do you feel confident in creating success?
- Do you empower others to take steps towards success?
- Do you feel blessed and grateful for all the positive changes you manifested?
- Do you take time to enjoy the impact of your manifestations?
- Do you accept that changes come with letting go of the past?
- Do you accept that others are not always happy with your new life style?
- Do you enjoy the impact of your positive thoughts, feelings and actions?

The Second Step

Analyze Your Home: Do You Experience Empowerment in Your Home or Office?

Acknowledge That Empowerment is Part of Your Life

To be an empowered human being is to be open to transformation in your life. When you start to change things, make the changes with the right attitude. Move forward without fear and even if you have fear, move forward anyway, even if your knees are knocking.

When you need to make changes in your life, make them without complaints; make them with the vision that it will help you to succeed in your goals.

Everything that empowered you, accept it with happiness and joy. People that criticize you unjustly do so because they wish to keep you small or close to them; have the courage to leave them behind and move forward on your path. Let go of things and people in a compassionate manner.

When something, or someone, is no longer helping you to attain your vision, it is sometimes time to move on. But you can leave them with grace and gratefulness. Never criticize them, just honor them on your path even if you had difficulties with them. Remember every one you met was there at the right time and in the right place for a perfect reason: your growth.

Obvious Signs That You Allow Empowerment in Your Life

When you enter your home you see that:

- You have images of powerful people displayed.
- You have images of the moments in your life that were empowering to you like receiving awards, trophies.
- You place ornaments, and move furniture with the right attitude. You know that using grace and gratitude as you make changes in your environment will create more power in your life.
- You have a tribute table where you display your awards and trophies.
- You display letters of recognition or pictures of you and famous and powerful people.
- You display front covers of major magazines with your name or face on them. Of course, if this doesn't exist yet, you can just make them up.

Extra Tips

☞ Always give yourself compliments when you look in the mirror.

☞ When others compliment you, accept their words with grace.

☞ When interviewers from TV and radio come to you, accept that you are becoming more powerful.

The Third Step

The Color of Empowerment—Cobalt Blue

Cobalt blue is the color of the night. The night is mysterious. When empowering games are played in fraternities and youth movements, they are done at night when the cobalt blue color surrounds everything. Have you ever tried to sneak out of home to go walking at night but you really had to tap into your inner power and be courageous just to conquer your fears.

You empowered yourself to go beyond your limits.

How Can You Use This Color?

☞ Place your awards, trophies, or items that connect you with courage on a cobalt blue fabric in the north area of your living room or bedroom.

☞ Especially for children that are bullied, place a picture of the child in a cobalt blue frame to create more inner power and strength.

Conclusion

You have known people that started in their lives as invisible young men and women; smart but unknown. First they had to empower themselves to believe that their own visions and goals were powerful. These young men and women had to overcome their own limitations to become great mentors and now empower others to fulfill their dreams.

EMPOWERMENT AFFIRMATIONS

I have the courage to make changes in my life.

I manifest the power that is in my professional life, my passion, and my vision.

I make changes with the right attitude.

I empower others to stand in their own power.

I am ready to manifest with ease and effortlessness.

Chapter 3

Do You Attract Wisdom?

I was raised Catholic in Belgium, so my first religious experiences were through Catholic rituals and church services. I remember that as a fifteen year old I wished to connect with someone very close to the pope as I saw him as the wisdom-keeper of my religion. I placed an image of the pope in the northeast area of my bedroom. I have to be honest though, when my girlfriends came over for slumber parties, I did hide that image. About one year later, the priest that was conducting the Catholic mass in my school invited me to his home.

He was almost eighty and he had noticed me because I sometimes played the piano to accompany the choir. When I entered his home I found that the exact same picture of the pope was also hung in his home.

He was a retired cardinal that worked in the Vatican in Rome and had been in close contact with the pope. Well, I thought, he can definitely give me some answers. He did, but also directed me on a path to open myself to other religions and see that God has many ways of expressing himself and that every way is Go(o)d.

The First Step
Analyze Your Life: Are You Attracting Wisdom?

Wisdom is a combination of intuition, inspiration, information, and knowledge.

I believe that it is an aspect that is not asked for enough. True wisdom is one of the greatest riches you can receive. It is actually not measurable in money: It is priceless. The Universe will not only provide you with wealth, happiness, and great health, you can also attract all the wisdom you need in your life. You may ask to have the wisdom to make the right decisions, to have discernment, to know exactly what to accept, and what to let go of.

This chapter is also about your spiritual or religious life. The very simple law of attraction is not connected with any religion, culture or race. It is a way of life that connects with every religion, spiritual practice, culture or race. It is non-judgmental and is full of compassion. Whatever you wish to attract, it is your responsibility and actually your decision. Nobody has the right to express any judgments to what you wish to attract and what you practice in your life.

Questions

- ☞ Do you feel inspired in your life?
- ☞ Do you create time for meditation or prayer?
- ☞ Do you have a mentor or a coach?
- ☞ Are you connected with a church or a spiritual practice?
- ☞ Do your dreams give you insight?
- ☞ Do you have contact with others who resonate with your ideas and your vision?
- ☞ Do you have a place in nature or in your home that you feel peaceful?
- ☞ Do you study, learn or remember easily?

The Second Step

Analyze Your Home: Do You Experience Wisdom in Your Home or Office?

A home does not have to be a temple unless you wish to live as a monk with no physical intimacy. If you do, I would suggest you fill your home with images of spirituality and religion. Still, there needs to be a place or certain area that gives you peace and inspiration. A person cannot live on money and love alone. We need time and a place to recharge our inner batteries. You need to let the Universe know that you are open to the Universal information that is out there for you.

When I enter a home or office I always look for signs that show me if the people there are connecting with their inner wisdom and if they are open to mentoring and teachers. If you wish to use the very simple law of attraction at its best you need to be teachable.

Every successful person I have met was involved in a spiritual or religious practice or believed in scientific knowledge. The European kings and queens, the emperors of China always had priests, advisors, or teachers around them. Great compassionate leaders know the value of wisdom.

I will give you a checklist of things to look for that can indicate that you are open to the knowledge or wisdom that the Universe can offer you, or if you are closing yourself from the treasures of the Universe. Are you awake to your inner voice or do you still sleep and have no connection with your inner being?

Acknowledge That Wisdom is Part of Your Life
Wisdom can be represented in many ways in your life.

To have wisdom it is necessary to attract mentors, coaches and teachers that will share their wisdom in your life. You also need time to reflect, to meditate, and to contemplate. Creating a space for wisdom is part of what you need to attract as well as make the time to go within, to pray, to do your affirmations, and to listen to your self-improvement CDs. You need to make time for seminars, classes and webinars, or web-seminars. Wisdom can be found in the words of elders, in books, in dreams, and in visions.

Obvious Signs That You Allow Wisdom in Your Life
When you enter your home you see that:
➴ You have a library that you use.
➴ You have meditation music playing in your home.

- You have images of angels, divine mothers, Buddha, Jesus, or any other divine statue hanging or standing in your home.
- You have a holy book within reach when you need it.
- You have an altar, a meditation area, a prayer chair.
- You have self-improvement CDs in your car.
- You have incense burning.
- You have a prayer candle lit for special requests.
- You have crystals in your home.
- You have a dream book next to your bed.

Enhance Your Connection With Heaven, the Universe or God

Activate Your Home for Wisdom

In the northeast area of your bedroom, living room or office, place a symbol, a book, an image that represents wisdom for you.

Activate Your Home for Mentorship

In the northwest area of your bedroom or living room, place a book, a picture, or CDs of your mentor, spiritual or religious advisor, psychologist or coach.

Activate Your Personal Wisdom Direction

In your personal wisdom direction place the book you are reading now, a flyer of the seminar you are going to attend, the master you devote your life to, or the music that inspires you. You can also hang the affirmation given to you in this area.

Extra Tips

- Always travel with an inspirational book.
- Include meditation or gospel music on your personal music player.
- Never sit with your back to the entrance: You wish to always be the master of your life from now on.

The Third Step
The Color of Wisdom—Yellow

The warm yellow of the sunlight brings us insights and wisdom. Yellow is a great color to have around you. It is one of my favorite colors to use in interior designs. It is wonderful to use in a child or teen room: They grow up to be wise young people.

How can you use this color?

- Place yellow flowers on your coffee table so that everyone in the home or office will react wisely in their communications.
- Wear as an outfit accessory color if you feel you can use this to support you in your power.
- Place a yellow item in the northeast area of your bedroom, office, or living room to attract more wisdom in your life.

Conclusion

Every successful person remains a student of life; they know that they will never know everything. They know that the more you know, the more there is to know. You will be more successful if you have the right attitude within yourself about wisdom, and allow wisdom to be displayed and attracted in your home and office.

WISDOM AFFIRMATIONS

I am an inspiration for others.

I receive wisdom for the next steps in my life.

I allow the right information to come to me to find solutions.

Chapter 4

Do You Attract Compassion?

In 1996 I traveled to Nepal with thirty-six students with the intent of visiting many Tibetan monasteries and also the Himalayas.

It was a challenging journey. I worked with a western woman who had helped to organize this trip; she knew the country and the people very well.

I found out on the trip that she knew them so well that she had organized extra deals behind my back to fill her pockets. One day we went to some local artists to buy Buddha statues. I wanted to give money directly to the artists supplying the shops instead of the shops. She arranged this for me and I was so happy that I asked everyone to give them the price they asked for and not to bargain, as it was still better than in the shops.

It was my way to give something back to the beautiful country and the people in Nepal. After visiting them, she stayed behind in the streets and I was worried and went back to search for her. I found her demanding payment from the artists because she had created revenues for them. She was already very well paid by me for the trip but she wanted extra cash. I was so shocked because the whole idea had been to not rip off these artisans and she had destroyed this with her greed.

At that moment a Tibetan monk dressed in his red and saffron yellow outfit crossed my path in the street. He smiled, looked at me and at her, and then said to me in English, "Buddha is compassionate." At that moment, my whole judgment towards this woman disappeared. Who was I to judge her, who was I to be shocked. Even when she showed up later that night bragging to everyone about the new outfits she had just bought with the money that I knew she received in payback, I complemented her on her beauty with grace, knowing that my intentions were pure and that she had still to learn her lesson about greed.

The First Step
Analyze Your Life: Are You Feeling Compassionate?

When you choose to change your life by attracting the right things, people and outcomes in your life, you need to start to feel compassionate about what you have attracted so far. When you start understanding what you have previously placed, hung, or colored in your home and office, and what it has done to your life, don't start judging yourself, but have compassion. You based your current life on what you knew. But now you can start transforming yourself and your environment based on your new information. You can't judge yourself for not knowing.

Questions

➤ Do you feel compassionate for yourself, for others and for the world you live in?

➤ Do you treat others with patience and gentleness?

➤ Do you open yourself to the advice of others?

➤ Do you listen to the life stories told by the elders of your community?

➤ Do you go easy on yourself when you try new things or make mistakes?

➤ Do you judge yourself for your past experiences or can you let go?

➤ Do you blame your parents or your husband or wife for your current life?

➤ Do you make excuses for yourself and your situation?

The Second Step
Analyze Your Home: Do You Experience Compassion in Your Home or Office?

Acknowledge That Compassion is Part of Your Life

A compassionate person will have no judgment unto themselves or others.

Especially when you know some Diamond Feng Shui tips, and you look around other people's homes, it is easy to start judging them for their lack of good Feng Shui. You can start laughing, and making remarks, when you see certain images that suggest they will not have romance for a while.

When entering people's homes and offices I learned to be full of compassion for what people have created in their lives. Still, it is important when you know that something is not supporting their lives or their goals, especially towards their children, that you insist they make the changes. When I see a child sleeping with a lot of images of war or fighting around them, or images with skulls or negative words, I insist they try to remove them and see how their child changes.

Obvious Signs That You Allow Compassion in Your Life
When You Enter Your Home You See:
- You have images or statues of the gods and goddesses that embody compassion in your home.
- You have books or movies about saints or people that stand for world peace or compassion such as Mother Theresa, Nelson Mandela, and Martin Luther King.
- You have items ready for donation to a good will organization in your area.
- You have a little bowl with coins that you give to those that beg when you see them on the street.
- You have removed all judgmental sentences, especially around children's rooms, such as: stay out, enter and you will be killed, etc.
- You have images of harmony hung around you.
- You have removed images of war and conflict.
- You have no images of people holding weapons.

☙ You have images or statues representing differing religions.

☙ You have books on opposing beliefs in your library.

☙ You have no images or statues of dead animals.

☙ You have no gossip magazines on display as they have no compassion for the lives of famous people.

Extra Tips

☙ Create soft area lighting when it gets darker outside.

☙ Place candles around your bath and make sure you use essential oils in your bathwater.

☙ Soft pillows and comfortable furniture will ease your life and create more compassion in your family life.

The Third Step
The Color of Compassion—Saffron Yellow

Saffron yellow is the color used by Tibetan Buddhist monks in their outfit.

Saffron is an herb that is used to harmonize food and the smell of this herb creates a mellow aroma that calms the business of life. Diamond Feng Shui is not connected with any religion, respect of all believes is just part of the compassionate attitude of Feng Shui. In comparing world religions you will find that Buddhism is an expression of faith that focuses very much on compassion.

The monks and nuns connected with this belief are seen as walking the path of compassion towards their fellow human beings. They honor life and are compassionate towards the animal kingdom to such a degree that the killing of any animal for pleasure or food is not allowed. They are compassionate to people and accordingly there is no judgment; it is just a different way of living your life.

How can you use this color?

➥ Paint your bedroom or living room in saffron yellow to create a more compassionate atmosphere, especially if a lot of fighting and bickering is happening in your relationship or family life.

➥ Place some saffron yellow pillows on the couch where you sit with people that are judging you.

➥ Place a bouquet of saffron yellow flowers between you and your judgmental colleague.

➥ Place a saffron yellow rug where you enter your home with the word "welcome" on it.

Conclusion

Life will get so much easier when you stop judging yourself and others. You lose so much energy when you judge others and it does not feel good in your heart. Today people love to hear the latest gossip about famous people.

They can talk all day about them and sometimes that information is in the news more than things that really matter to our lives. I learned to say that, "When you walk in their shoes or boots or high heels for a mile, perhaps you will speak differently."

COMPASSION AFFIRMATIONS

I practice the path of compassion.

May my love enlighten my path.

May I be carried by the compassion
of others on my path.

May the compassion of the Universe
embrace my path.

I am ready to compassionately manifest
my vision on my path.

Chapter 5

~~~~~~

Do You
Attract Love?

When I was eighteen years old I had a wonderful relationship but after that summer I didn't attract a boyfriend for several years. I had many girlfriends but not one romance. It was as if I couldn't even see that they were looking at me. My girlfriends told me many times, "Marie, are you blind, it is like you don't see that they are interested in you." Interestingly, I started drawing intensely when I was eighteen years old and the images I drew over and over again were of women with one eye. The other eye was covered by long hair. I created a series of these portraits and called them "The Muses."

I did hang them above my bed and indeed I attracted many slumber parties with my girlfriends in that room but no boyfriend. How could I? I indicated to the Universe I wanted to be surrounded by girlfriends. There was not one image of a couple hanging anywhere. Plus I had mirrors across from my bed doubling the girlfriends. I knew about Feng Shui but I didn't understand all the consequences yet of what I placed around me. When I was twenty-six years old I replaced them with images of couples and about six months later I found my husband, to whom I am still happily married.

The First Step
Analyze Your Life: Are You Feeling Loved?

The word love and the word law are of the same origin. The law of the Universe is love and it starts right with you. Do you love yourself? I am not speaking about adoring what you wear, how you look, and the clothes you wear, but do you love who you are, what you are doing, and the life that you created? When you give love to yourself, you will start receiving love from others. Love is a flow of energy. When you want it to appear in your life, you must start sharing with yourself and with others.

Questions
- Do you feel love in your heart?
- Do you create time for your loved ones?
- Do you have loving relationships with your parents?
- Are you connected with your family?
- Do your share your dreams with friends?
- Do you feel you can be yourself with the people that you love?

👄 Do you have a place in your home where you can make love?

👄 Do you have great collaboration with your colleagues?

The Second Step

Analyze Your Home: Do You Experience Love in Your Home or Office?

Love is in the air. It is so true. In certain homes you feel the love hanging around. You don't want to leave that place because the whole atmosphere breaths love; the smell, the colors, the coziness, the warmth of the people welcoming you. Even in a shop or an office love can be in the air when people are selling products they love. Have you ever walked into a shop where people don't like what they are selling? You can feel that and you don't go back. But if you enter a shop where they love their products and they are so happy to sell you something, not because of the incoming money, but because they love to make people happy with the products they sell; you will want to go back again. From the moment that you enter a home, you need to feel the love in the air. If you don't feel it in your own home, don't be surprised that you don't attract lovely relationships in your home.

Acknowledge That Love is a Part of Your Life

Love can be represented in many ways in your life.

Remember that I said that first of all you have to have love for yourself. You also need to activate the love in the relationships with your past or current family. Love in your romantic relationships is of course something that people dream about: Where is the princess that I need to rescue me from the dragon and where is the prince on the white horse? If you're not ready, your prince or princess will not come. You can also attract more general lovely relationships that will support you through thick and thin like good friends.

Giving love and receiving love from your children and grandchildren is always part of a loving life.

Obvious Signs That You Allow Love in Your Life

When you enter you home you see that:

- You have many pictures of you and your family—make sure you are in the pictures.
- If you have children, make sure you have their drawings hanging and a box of toys always ready to be used.
- You have images of romantic couples or your own wedding pictures have a central place in the living room and bedroom.
- You have items in pairs to send a message of positive relationships.
- You have a team picture hanging up.
- The Chinese double happiness symbol is in a strategic place in your home.

Enhance Your Love Connections

Activate Your Personal Romantic Relationships

In the southwest area of your bedroom and living room place a symbol, a book, or an image that represents your personal relationship.

Activate Your Relationships With Your Children and Grandchildren

In the west area of your living or family room place their pictures, their drawings, or the toys of your small ones. You can also place there, ornaments related to children such as an image of children playing.

Activate Your Relationships With Your Friends

In the northwest area of your living room place images of you and your friends, your address book, or a statue of a friendship circle.

Activate Your Relationships With Your Family

In the east area of your living or family room place images of your family; a family symbol, coat of arms, and a family tree can be supportive.

Activate Your Personal Relationship Direction

You can also place personal images of your relationships, especially the ones that can use some extra care, in your personal best relationship direction.

You can also hang the affirmations in this area.

Extra Tips

☞ Always travel with pictures of your loved ones.

☞ Place an image of the people that live with you at the entrance to show them that each time they enter the home they are very welcome.

☞ If your wish is to never be alone in your life, then make sure that when you are in pictures you are always with others.

The Third Step
The Color of Love—Rose

I am sure it is no surprise to anyone that the color of love is rose. I am sure that the rose is the flower that is given to people the most for Valentine's Day and to celebrate relationships. Do you also look through rose-colored glasses when you are in love and do you have rose butterflies in your belly?

How can you use this color?

☞ When you have a meeting with a loved one, give them a rose. Love will be in the air, guaranteed. Red roses don't do the same trick, they will create passionate intimacy but rose stands for unconditional love. Love without expectations.

☞ Place rose flowers at the entrance to your garden so everyone will feel welcome and love even before they walk in to your home.

☞ Place a rose colored item in the southwest area of your bedroom, office or living room to attract more love in your life.

Conclusion

If you haven't had enough love in the air, start spreading rose mist or use rose essential oil in your bath to attract love. Start loving yourself and others will fall in love with you too. But you need to start first by falling in love with you. You can't expect your parents to love you if you don't love being their child. You can't expect your romantic partner to love you if you don't love to be her husband or his wife. You can't expect your friends to love you when you don't love being their friends. So start loving by placing images that reflect love, and items symbolically expressing the quality of love in yourself and for others in your home.

LOVE AFFIRMATIONS

I am in love with a wonderful partner.

I create lovely relationships with
my family and friends.

I allow myself to be open to receive love.

Chapter 6

Do You Attract Tenderness?

When I am on a holiday or take a get-away weekend, then I really focus on being tender to myself. It may start with going to a great hotel where they have smooth carpets to walk on, or linens that are soft and smell nice. A view from the balcony that overlooks a beautiful valley or the ocean is always nice. I like to go to a wonderful restaurant where I can smell all the delicious food that is prepared by a great chef and brought by a waiter that knows the menu and how to give pampering service. Luxury can feel like tenderness. After my ego level is satisfied with being treated tenderly, I am ready to let my soul feel the tenderness of the Universe.

One day I experienced the luxury version of tenderness. I was invited aboard one of the largest yachts in St. Tropez in the South of France. My senses felt so happy:

there was great food and I was surrounded by beauty and the ocean. A week later I was invited to the apartment of a friend near the Mont Blanc. It was the opposite of beauty in her home. It was a typical French apartment. She was very welcoming but the smell of mold and the grayness of her walls was such a shock to my senses. I decided to go for a hike to the mountains to touch base with the tenderness of nature. I ended up in a bad storm and had to sleep at a local farm. The welcoming family gave me bread and fresh cheese, a warm fire and a night in the barn above the cows, where the cats warmed me up to protect me from the rats and mice. I can tell you that night my heart was full of real tenderness for this family and for nature and all its smells. Walking down the mountain after the fresh storm, my senses were the clearest they have ever been. I felt touched by the grace of the Universe in me and around me.

The First Step
Analyze Your Life: Are You Feeling Tender?

When I hear "Love Me Tender," the famous song sung by Elvis Presley, I always feel so tender in my heart. Sweet voices can really touch me. What makes one tender will be different for many people. But somehow that song allowed people in this western masculine culture to bring tenderness into their lives. If the King of Rock and Roll was allowed to be tender so were all men; this song did something to the consciousness of the western world.

I feel that today we still need to take time for tenderness to our bodies, our minds, and souls. A lot of products and treatments are out there to create tenderness to our physical body. But let's be honest, the mind is oversaturated with a constant flow of information and technical gadgets.

Even in the elevator or in the line of the supermarket you get information downloads. Tenderness is sometimes hidden in the silence. Less is definitely more when we wish to be tender to ourselves.

Questions

- Do you allow yourself to be touched tenderly by your loved ones?
- Do you allow children or grandchildren to play funny tender games with you?
- Do you wear silk or soft cotton or wool on your body?
- Do you allow people to massage your body or rub your feet?
- Do you give personalized gifts?
- Do you give with yourself to others with your heart?
- Do you write love letters or little notes to be read at breakfast?
- Do you look at your watch in anticipation when you are meeting a loved one?

The Second Step
Analyze Your Home: Do You Experience Tenderness in Your Home or Office?

Acknowledge That Tenderness is Part of Your Life

Obvious Signs That You Allow Tenderness in Your Life
When You Enter Your Bedroom You See:

☞ Items in pairs like two hearts, two candles, and images of couples.

☞ You see images of angels.

☞ You have soft and sensuous fabrics on your bed.

☞ You have pillows in pastel colors or heart-shaped pillows.

☞ When you step out of bed there is a warm and soft carpet under your feet.

☞ Your alarm or wakeup call is soft music.

☞ Your mirrors are covered, as they stop tender intimacy for the couple.

☞ You have images of smiling people around you.

Extra Tip
☞ You have stuffed animals around you on your bed.

When You Enter Your Garden
☞ You have a wind chime hanging in your garden that gives you a tender background sound.

☞ You have different flower pots with bees buzzing around them.

- You have a birdbath or a bird feeder.
- You have a waterfall in your garden giving you sooth-ing sounds.
- You have crystals that reflect the intense sunlight in your windows creating rainbows.

Extra Tip

- You have images of fairies, gnomes, dragon flies, or but-terflies in your garden.

The Third Step

The Color of Tenderness—Pink

We know that touching the skin of a newborn baby is the tenderest feeling in the world. When a baby of any race is born it has the softest blush of life. That kind of tender-ness is evoked when we bring the color pink into our lives.

How can you use this color?

- Wear a pink nightgown or underwear. For men, a pink shirt will help them to bring forward the tender aspect of themselves.
- Place a bouquet of pink roses on your dining room table.
- You can also hang images of pink flowers in the hall-ways leading to your bedroom.

Conclusion

After a period of wearing a lot of dark colors for my work, I craved pink. I bought everything I could in this color. Actually, while writing this chapter I have on a soft pink outfit. With the sound of the outside fountain and the background ring of a wind chime, I feel as if I am in heaven.

TENDERNESS AFFIRMATIONS

I create tenderness for myself
and my loved ones.

I allow my skin to feel tender clothing.

I allow my eyes to see sweet and tender images.

I allow my nose to smell sweet scents.

I allow my ears to hear
harmonious sounds and voices.

Chapter 7

Do You Attract Purity?

I once lived for two years in a home where the energy was not pure. This home had seen some sad moments in the past: the former owner had drowned in the ocean. The entrance of the home was on the north side and surrounded by many high trees; enough light would come in only in the summer. It was a dark home. I felt very depressed there, I couldn't focus and we had the most cluttered home. After a while I started adding lamps and candlelight in the corners. I changed my dark couches for white sofas. I started wearing white and pastel colored outfits and I began feeling so much better. I was focused again and my home looked neat. I found a cleaning product with lavender essential oil in it and I used it to clean everything. The aura field of the home became bright as I spread lavender mist around me every day. I even started to like the home. It became very clear to me what I wanted to do with my life and after we left that home my career as a self- improvement teacher began.

The First Step
Analyze Your Life: Are You Feeling Pure?

When you have already changed your home to use the law of attraction, but you have not received any major changes, you may need to take care of the level of purity that is in your home. Purity stands for the level of light that you have in your home or office. Universal energy is reflected in the white light of the sun and you need to have a certain amount of real light in your home. If there is no way that you can have real sunlight entering you need to fake it and ensure that you use electrical light in dark areas of your home.

Questions

- Do you open the windows and doors to bring in light and activate your senses?
- Do you feel abusive, or abused by others?
- Do you have a hard time setting your own boundaries for others?
- Do you repair things quickly when they need it?
- Do you display broken things?
- Do you wash your body every day?
- Do you remember the last time you did a spring clean up of your home?
- Do you let go of clutter easily?

The Second Step
Analyze Your Home: Do You Experience Purity in Your Home or Office?

Acknowledge That Purity is Part of Your Life

The Universe needs a vessel to bring in the gifts. Light is a vessel of transportation. The quality of light in your home or office will influence the ease with which the Universe can bring in your requests. Here, the word light means more than visual light. It also refers to whether the etheric field of your home feels light. You can feel this if you enter some where and you feel as if you can't breathe there; you feel uneasy, something is bothering you. You can't really tell what it is but you feel that something is not right. It is the aura field in the home that has a lower level of energy. When you live in such an aura field, you will start feeling down and depressed yourself. The more clutter and the more lack of light you have, the more you will feel uninspired and unhappy. As you feel this, so will the Universe react to you.

Obvious Signs That You Allow Purity in Your Life

- When you walk in your home, you feel a sense of relief: You are home.
- You are open to new ideas; self-help books and creativity books are on your book table.
- You have lights in all the four corners of your living room: There are no dark areas.
- You have no broken objects displayed.

☛ You keep up with all the home repairs.

☛ Your blinds are not closed; you allow the sunlight to enter your home.

☛ You have a place to meditate or pray or to read; a place of retreat.

☛ You have images of joy, sun, beaches, flowers etc., hung in your home. There are no images of thunder, storms, ravines, or winter in your home.

Extra Tips

☛ Add lavender essential oil to your cleaning products.

☛ Dust your furniture every week.

☛ Remove the spider webs.

The Third Step
The Color of Purity—White

When you look at different cultures and religions, white is used to show a new beginning. For baptisms, marriages, and even deaths, they use the color white. Using white is the moment when people try to be pure of intention, when the entire ego disappears. The moment is important and all the negative feelings are gone. In Diamond Feng Shui, I suggest that people wear white more often especially around the heart, even if it is only a bra.

So, at least around the heart center we have a color that helps us to stay pure in our intentions.

How can you use this color?

➤ You can place a white object in the west area of your living room, office, and bedroom.

➤ Place some white flowers on your coffee table.

➤ Hang an image of a white angel above or near the front door to tell the Universe your choice is to have an uplifting pure energy field.

Conclusion

Remember that when the Universe is not returning your calls, or not fulfilling your orders, don't start doubting or blaming. Just clean up and uplift the light level of your home. The more light there is inside, the better the Universal delivery plane will know where to deliver.

PURITY AFFIRMATIONS

I give myself permission to place
my own boundaries.

I let go of all abusive behavior
in myself and by others.

I am attracting purity in my thoughts,
feelings and actions.

I move forward towards my goals
with pure intentions.

Chapter 8

Do You Attract Transparency?

Focusing on transparency is a constant issue. When I feel blocked or I feel things are not moving like I want, I feel like I want to clean up my office, a closet, or my computer. It feels great to release old stuff and to create space for new gifts from the Universe. When I was young, I loved to go in old garages and storage places and throw everything out. Then I asked my family what they still wanted. Turning a chaotic place in to a place of order and beauty is one of my favorite things to do. In this case you need to do it yourself; I am not coming over to help you.

What I liked about it the most were the treasures I found, like the old pictures, and then deciding what I still wanted in my life. The last seventeen years I have moved about twelve times and my favorite part of moving is getting to clean things up before I move. And if I'm not moving I still have these monthly urges to clean up a closet or a room. If you do things regularly your life will keep moving towards your goal. No goals can be attained if your environment is full of clutter and chaos.

The First Step

Analyze Your Life: Are You Feeling Transparent?

In order to manifest with speed you need to make the aura field of your home transparent so you can see the gifts coming in to your life. To me some homes feel as if there is smog hanging in and around them. How can you see what gifts the Universe is bringing in the air if the space is full of old energy?

The law of attraction can only really work if you prepare yourself to receive the manifestation of your wishes. When cleaning up your inner self we really don't know how much there is to clean up, but your home is a good reflection of the chaos inside yourself. If there is clutter and disorganization in your home, I can guarantee you there are emotions and ideas that are blocking you on the inside. By cleaning and de-cluttering the outside, your inside will start to change as well.

Questions

➣ Do you feel disorganized?

➣ Do you allow people to come to dinner or is there no place available at your table because of the clutter?

➣ Do you use a lot of perfume or mists to create a better smell in your home?

➣ Do you dare open a closet?

❧ Is your computer getting overloaded by too many files?
❧ Do you tidy up at night so you can start fresh in the morning?
❧ Have you opened your windows lately to bring in fresh air?
❧ Do people find their way to your home or apartment?

The Second Step
Analyze Your Home: Do You Experience Transparency in Your Home or Office?

Acknowledge That Transparency is Part of Your Life
In order to receive the gifts from the Universe you need to create an open landing space for the Universal delivery airplane to land on the ground.

I enter homes sometimes in which you can feel that the energy closed to Universe bringing in gifts; the requests of the people living there. It is hard for me to breathe in such a place, so why would the Universal mailman come by?

Where there is no open space, you cannot receive.

Obvious Signs That You Allow Transparency in Your Life
❧ When you walk in your home, your first view is clean and uplifting.
❧ All non-decorative items are stored in boxes, drawers, or cabinets.
❧ When you open the fridge, old food and expired food has been discarded.
❧ Your windows are clean and you can see through them.

* There are no hairs from animals on your couch.
* There are no books lying around.
* Sick and old plants are removed.
* Your garbage bins are not overflowing.
* You can walk around the furniture.

Extra Tips
* Open the windows every week to bring in fresh air.
* Keep your pool and Jacuzzi free of leaves.

The Third Step
The Color of Transparency—Ivory

It is said that elephants remember everything that happened in their lives, especially the negative experiences. An African shaman once told me that everything is stored in their ivory teeth. The cleaner their teeth are, the less scars they have, the more they were free of negative vibrations. I don't know the truth about this, but I do know that a home keeps track of negative vibrations. A home has a memory too and some people can feel it and even see the scar in the energy field of a home. Don't add more negative vibrations; let the wind take them outside.

How can you use this color?
* You can place transparent glass items around you and place your flowers in transparent vases.
* You can place some ivory white sea salt in the corners of every room of your home. Keep it there for seven days to clear out the energetic negative vibrations.

Conclusion

Transparency for certain people and for certain homes is a constant focus.

This is especially true when several people live in a home or use the same bathroom or work on the same computer. The more you create physical transparency in your home, the more emotional, mental, and spiritual you will feel. You will be transparent and free of negative feelings, ideas, and vibrations.

TRANSPARENCY AFFIRMATIONS

I de-clutter my life and create order.

I uplift the world around me
so I feel uplifted inside me.

I organize my life to bring it to the next level.

I let go of what doesn't serve me anymore.

I allow transparency to come
into my environment.

I open my heart to receive
spiritual transparency.

Chapter 9

Do You Attract Health?

When I was fifteen years old I had a major accident. I survived but with a lot of health issues; only twenty percent of my short term memory worked. For about ten years I was more often in bed than out and health was a real issue until I was twenty-five years old. I had the good fortune to live in a home surrounded by trees and a beautiful garden. Whenever I felt low energy I walked in the garden to connect with the trees and the flowers. But in retrospective I did something else that at that time I didn't understand very well. I really wanted to wear green outfits a lot; especially when I had to study for tests. For ten years my favorite outfit was an emerald green short skirt and polo shirt. Otherwise I never wore such colors. Even today, green is not one of my major colors. As you read on you will understand that emerald green is a healing color and creates good health for us. It is the color of nature where all the healing power is.

The First Step
Analyze Your Life: Are You Feeling Healthy?

In the traditional Chinese culture good health is seen as more important than great romance. That is why the Chinese take such a good care of them selves by doing Tai Chi or Qi Qong, or taking traditional Chinese herbs. Longevity itself is a goal of many Chinese people. You only start understanding how important health is when you start losing it. A home can definitely inspire good health. The ancient Feng Shui Masters bring two aspects together to create good health: having good Feng Shui and sleeping or living where there is no geopathic stress. The ancient paintings showed Feng Shui masters with a compass and a dowsing rod. Dowsing is not part of this book, but it might be something to check out if even after following some Diamond Feng Shui tips, your health is not improving. Perhaps you have been sleeping on a fault line, or there is water running under your home. Even good Feng Shui cannot cure those problems.

Questions

➤ Have you had problems with your health lately?

➤ Do you wish to attract the right solutions for maintaining your health?

➤ Do you wish to attract the right therapy to keep you balanced?

➤ Are you a member of a good gym or sports center?

➤ Have you had major surgery since you moved in?

➤ Have you had any of accidents since you moved in?

- Do you feel emotionally sane and mentally peaceful where you live?
- Do you feel balanced in what you do?

The Second Step
Analyze Your Home: Do You Experience Health in Your Home or Office?

Acknowledge That Health is Part of Your Life.

Health can be represented in many ways in your life.

To have health you need to make sure you are in balance. When you overdo in one area of your life you don't have enough energy for the other areas. Most women and men today are focused on success and relationships. Health is not one of their favorite topics until they hit a rock on their path. That rock can mentally overwhelm, emotionally depress, cause sudden physical problems, or be a life threatening disease. Feng Shui is about balance between yin and yang; passive and active; night and day. You need to balance the active part and the passive part of your life. You need time to sleep and relax. All the hours that you don't relax will accumulate and before you know it you will create something in your health where you must start to relax and catch up on the sleep hours you have been missing.

In order to have great health you also need to have the right health team in place around you; the best doctor, healer, masseuse, chiropractor, etc. If you don't need them, great, but if you do, you need the best that are available. Part of focusing on great health is also attracting the right people to support you with this.

Health is also about prevention by taking supplements, using a healthy diet, walking in nature, doing breathing exercises, meditation, or anything that can keep your health perfect.

Obvious Signs That You Allow Health in Your Life

When you enter your home and you see that:

* You have a balance between passive and active areas in your home. Certain rooms are quiet and others are active.
* You have the five elements in your home: water, wood, fire, earth, and metal.
* You have images of lush green, flowers, and gardens. Do not display plants with pointy leaves.
* You always have the bathroom door closed so the flushing energy of the toilet is not connected with the living areas.
* You can hear the sounds of birds or wind chimes.
* You have books on healing and therapy on your night stand.
* You have images of people walking, running, or doing exercises hanging—but not in your bedroom.
* You always have fresh flowers in your home; never dead flowers or potpourri.
* You have stored away all sharp objects and weapons.
* You have no heads of dead animals hanging on the walls.
* You have placed all garbage bins in a closet.

Activate the Health of Your Whole Family

In the east area of your family or living room place a bamboo or lush green plant.

Activate Balance

Play soft background music and place a crystal on the coffee table by your couches.

Activate Your Home to Attract a Good Health Team

In the northwest area of your bedroom or living room place information or the business cards of the team that will help you create excellent health.

Activate Your Personal Health Direction

In your personal health direction place more personal information about your health; your medicine and supplements, books about healing, etc. You can also hang the affirmations in this area.

Extra Tips

☞ Always travel with healing tapes to listen to.

☞ Open the windows an hour before you go to sleep to let in fresh air.

☞ Walk daily to create balance between your yin and yang.

The Third Step
The Color of Health—Emerald Green

Emerald green is the color that inspires health. It relates to nature and the source of health we experience by connecting with the treasures that are in nature: air, herbs, quietness, relaxation.

How can you use this color?

- Place lush green plants in your living room or family room. Make sure you don't place them in your bedroom as they create too much active energy within the passive environment that the nighttime needs.
- Wear emerald green as an accessory color if you feel you can use this color to support your health.
- Place a green item in the east area of your bedroom, office, or living room to attract more good health in your life.

Conclusion

When you feel that success is slowing down, it is perhaps because your health is slowing down. When your relationships are not so sparkling anymore, it is possible that your health is not that sparkling anymore either. So if you feel that things are not going so well for you always stimulate your health.

HEALTH AFFIRMATIONS

I am healing with ease.

I receive the right information
to heal my body.

I attract the right help
to solve my health issues.

I am in great health in my mind,
body, and spirit.

Chapter 10

Do You Attract Honesty?

Many years ago I was invited to a wedding celebration. I had been teaching for several years and many of my students were also invited; that night I felt I wanted to wear citrus green, the color of honesty. So I shopped until I found a gorgeous outfit. What I didn't know was that some of my male students wanted to test me to see if I was a true master. The table was set up in such a way that my husband and I were separated. I was sitting between two male students and my husband was between two of my female students; I immediately felt very uneasy. Within a half hour these two gentlemen began touching me inappropriately and the two women did the same thing to my husband. I became very angry and insisted that I sit with my husband. I told them how dishonorable they were to play that game with me. I know wearing that color allowed me to see the dishonesty of this evening faster.

The First Step
Analyze Your Life: Are You Being Honest?

Being honest is about being truthful to your highest self. Why are you here in this world? The world honor is in this word. In China the code of honor is connected with dragons. Being a dragon you follow the codes of honor that you ask of yourself, or that a community, or elder, or master asks of you. The Universe has its codes of honor too. They are called the laws of the Universe. When you honor them you will receive honest answers. It is quite simple. Follow the codes of honor of the Universe and you will receive the power and abundance of a dragon and according to Chinese legends that is definitely unlimited power and abundance.

Questions

- Do you feel honored in your life?
- Do you play the game of the Universe honestly?
- Do you set priorities for what you have to do next?
- Do you think, do, and say the right things?
- When the flow of life is not great, do you check your behavior and adjust it?
- Do you use your talents for the greatest good?
- Do you check with a mentor to see if you are still on track?
- Do you keep track of your records?

The Second Step
Analyze Your Home: Do You Experience Honesty in Your Home or Office?

Acknowledge That Honor is Part of Your Life
Honesty is simply about following some rules. Unfortunately we make up so many excuses with our ego; we always have a reason to say it is too hard, too much discipline, and too much work. When you connect with the honor in yourself and keep true to your vision and to the laws of the Universe, everything will work out.

Obvious Signs That You Allow Honesty in Your Life
☛ You have images or statues of dragons in your home.
☛ You have images of statues of elephants and dinosaurs in your house—these reflect honesty too.
☛ You keep the center of your home open and spacious.
☛ You do not have heavy furniture in the center area.
☛ You have images of honorable people visible in your home.
☛ You have images or books connected with honorable causes such as nonprofit organizations, or Greenpeace, or AIDS research and care, visible in your home.
☛ You don't hang fake art work. What you hang is from original artists.

Extra Tips
☛ Remove covers from your sofas or couches.
☛ It is better to hang nothing than something that reflects something negative.

The Third Step
The Color of Honesty—Citrus
Have you ever tried to lie about something when you are eating a lemon?

Citrus, in my native Dutch language is close to "citroen," which translates as "lemon." Drinking water with lemon in the morning helps to clean your body of everything that is not honoring it. It helps to detoxify you.

How can you use this color?
- In the east area of your living room you can place citrus green images or items.
- Wear a citrus green outfit if you wish to find out the truth about a situation.

Conclusion
Honor yourself and others will honor you. At the very least, the Universe/

God will honor you with the gifts you have asked for. If you don't feel that doing that is very easy then breathe like a dragon and you will start understanding what you need to do to be truthful to your vision and goals.

HONESTY AFFIRMATIONS

I am honest with myself.

I hold my self accountable for
my intentions and my actions.

I stay true to my vision.

I accept that my friends can be honest with me.

Chapter 11

Do You Attract Balance?

One of the important benefits of Diamond Feng Shui is a deep sense of balance. When I came to live in the United States I didn't have a lot of furniture for my family. Being a first generation immigrant and trying to make my dreams come true created a lot of stress for me. Many times my family and I were ready to stop the adventure and go back home. The times when I saw black snow and didn't have enough money for food and clothing are not that long ago. At one point some friends donated a pair of ruby red couches to us. I always felt that these ruby red colored big one-seaters created balance for my family. Just by looking at them it made me feel that everything was worth doing. Now that these years of barely surviving are done I still have these couches, and they remind me of the times when balance was all I had.

The First Step
Analyze Your Life: Are You Feeling Balanced?

Balance is in the field of energy between active energy which equals Yang and passive energy which equals Yin. It is an awareness of being that is said to be experienced by the enlightened ones; the yogis, the masters. Most people experience balance when there is peace in their mind and heart. It is the combination of a passive environment where silence and stillness is experienced along with the activeness of the heart and mind. Your heart is able to love and your mind is able to inspire. Most people experience balance when they are on holiday and are not involved in the active energy of their work anymore. They are active enough to walk and exercise but are not subject to the daily stress of performance. When a person's life is balanced they feel happy inside and also happy with what is around them.

Questions

- Do you feel balanced between your outside life and inside life?
- Do you create a lot of conflicts with others?
- Do you still have old conflicts with family members of friends?
- Do you stop conflicts from escalating?
- Do you have balance in your body?
- Do you experience mood swings?
- Are you extreme in your principles?
- Do you feel energetic and at the same time relaxed?

The Second Step
Analyze Your Home: Do You Feel Balanced in Your Home or Office?

Acknowledge That Balance is Part of Your Life

So you see even when you and your life are already fairly well balanced, Diamond Feng Shui will extend your personal experience of balance in more energetic and spiritual ways. When people want success, energy, passionate relationships, and unlimited inspiration from the Universe at all times then they are in for a surprise as the Universe balances things out. You need time when you can enjoy the success you created, you need time to create that high physical energy level, you need time to enjoy the passion you experienced and you need time to study and connect with your mentors so you can be ready for the next level of inspiration. That is why there will be times that the Universe is not giving you anything more than down time; because that is just what you need so the next level can happen. So you see, the Universe knows exactly what you need to attain your goals. When nothing happens, know that it is part of the manifestation. But perhaps you need to balance some things before you can receive.

Obvious Signs That You Allow Balance in Your Life

- You display a yin-yang symbol.
- You have ruby reds in your interior design.
- You have all five elements in your environment: water, wood, fire, earth, and metal.

- You have an L-shaped, U-shaped, or T-shaped form of a home and you have balanced it with lights and by adding patios or gardens.
- You have nothing standing higher than your eye level on cupboards or on cabinets.
- You have everything in pairs or even numbers such as two, four, or six chairs.
- You do not have a staircase or a bathroom in the centre of your home.
- You do not have carpets that you can fall over.
- You don't have a tower of books that is ready to fall down.
- Toys and clothing are stored properly and are not left lying around.

Extra Tips

- Do not put water and fire together unless you wish to create a clash of imbalance.
- Make sure your fridge is filled with balanced food like veggies and fruits.

The Third Step

The Color of Balance—Ruby Red

The ruby is a gemstone that helps create balance in your life. The deep red color is sometimes used to balance the white of the yang energy and the black of the yin energy. That is why the combination of red, white, and black is so popular.

How can you use this color?

☞ You can place ruby red place mats on the table to create balance in your family.

☞ You can place a ruby red item in the south area of your office or bedroom.

☞ You can give your beloved something in a ruby gem-stone to help them balance their life.

Conclusion

Balance is the platform of success; it is something to pray for. We are in awe of people in the circus that can balance above the ground, but we should be in awe of people in balance on the ground.

BALANCE AFFIRMATIONS

I have the insights to make the right decision.

I can resolve conflicts that I created in the past.

I focus on balance with my family
and in my home.

I open myself to attract balanced
people and situations.

Chapter 12

Do You Attract Passion?

Perhaps you have seen the movie *The Secret* or read the book. I am featured in the section about relationships. Before I did my interview I meditated for about two hours and I asked the Universe what color I should have around me. People that know me personally know that I am very passionate about what I bring in to the world. In this case I felt that I wanted to let people know how passionately I want to share Universal knowledge and wisdom with them so their lives would become happier.

So I chose to wear a cherry red outfit. It was so red that even today people think I had red hair at the time of the movie. It was blond, but I think my aura field was a passionate cherry red. After the interview Rhonda Byrne told me I would be in the movie because I transcended the screen with passion for what I shared. People still remember me today for the red outfit I wore the day of filming. The cherry red definitely did its trick.

The First Step
Analyze Your Life: Are You Feeling Passionate?

I am passionate about colors and unfortunately I don't see enough of that passion reflected in the environment of this western world. Forms, colors, shapes, and fabric reflect the beauty of the Universe. I do see that many people don't see themselves or their homes as a reflection of the Universe, because the Universe is definitely not as dull as many people show in their homes. I am happy to be from Europe where I grew up with different architectural styles and ancient beauty. In North America I feel that when I enter someone's home I can use my passion to empower them where they live. The first thing I need to bring forward are colors to change the dullness of a home. I ask them to open up their drawers and cabinets and bring out their beautiful china and fabrics and I show them how to use their belongings in the right way.

Questions
☙ Do you feel passionate about your life?
☙ Do you use colors in your outfit or do you wear a typical black costume?
☙ Is your life dull or do you have a passion that you really enjoy?
☙ Are you a boring personality or a flamboyant soul?

- Do you express yourself in everything you do or do you let others take the lead?
- Do you still have pillow fights?
- Are you recognized on the street because of your radiant look?
- Does your smile open people's hearts?

The Second Step
Analyze Your Home: Do You Feel Passionate in Your Home or Office?

Acknowledge That Passion is Part of Your Life

Without passion there is no drive. It is your fuel that makes your dream move forward. Dreams without passion don't happen. If you want your wish and your request to the Universe to manifest you need to let the Universe know that you are passionate about it; not only by thinking and feeling but by acting upon it to show the Universe that this is what you wish for.

Obvious Signs That You Allow Passion in Your Life

- You display large images of what you are passionate about; small items will not do it.
- You have reds in your interior design.
- You have all five elements in your environment: water, wood, fire, earth and metal.
- You have passionate images in your bedroom.
- You have flowers and fruit out in your dining room.

- You use colorful table runners, napkins, and pillows.
- You place images of your passion on the walls.
- You have the tools of your passion standing, hanging, and displayed in your environment.

Extra Tips
- Don't display too many water images or you will cool the passion.
- Make sure your fridge is at least half full and there are healthy fruits and vegetables.

The Third Step
The Color of Passion—Cherry Red

Have you ever seen a couple in love eating fresh cherries together? One holds the cherry up while the other reaches for it with their lips. It shows that they are living passionately. They live their life with great intensity.

Cherry red is the color of intensity and knowing that you can make more of this life than you originally imagined.

How can you use this color?
- You can place images of your romantic relationship in a cherry red frame.
- You can use cherry red colors at your dinner party.
- You can wear a special red dress for a flamboyant dance party.

Conclusion

I would encourage you to live life with more passion. You don't have to live as if you are living the last day of your life; but do what you do with passion.

If you don't do that already then now is the time to change something in your life. Perhaps you can start by changing your attitude towards life. Find something you love and feel like you live it in every cell of your body.

PASSION AFFIRMATIONS

I feel passionate in my life.

I uplift the world around me
so I feel uplifted inside me.

I inspire passion in others.

I open myself to a colored life.

I allow forms and colors to give my life energy.

I open my heart to receive
spiritual transparency.

Chapter 13

Do You Attract Forgiveness?

When I started to become a self-help teacher and a Feng Shui expert, I needed to let go of my career as a lawyer. I really needed to let go of the patterns that I had created in that world. I chose one day to buy a violet colored car to drive in to all my classes and events. Each time I drove it I imagined that I did let go of all my old patterns and behaviors in myself and with others. It was a great car and it brought me many changes. Later when I came to live in the United States, I didn't have my violet car but I did have a violet shawl that I would wear day and night. I felt that I needed it around me all the time. I had to let go of many attachments with European culture, and was in the process of letting go of family and friends so I could open myself to new friends.

After two years of wearing this shawl I suddenly felt comfortable in myself with the life I had created here and I never wore that shawl again; it had served its purpose.

The First Step
Analyze Your Life: Are You Able to Forgive?

In order to create new space and new opportunities to come to your life you need to let go of the past. On an emotional level we call this forgiveness, on the level of a home you call this space clearing. When it is hard to do emotional forgiving, I suggest you start with doing space clearing on different levels; not only physical, but also energetic space clearing. The material surrounding us that we live in is not just what we see. It is not only matter; it has an aura field around it. In that aura field the emotional vibrations are captured. Space clearing helps you to let go of not only the objects connected with the past but also the energy that we created and is hanging around us that needs to be cleansed.

Questions

- Do you feel your life in the past more than in the present moment?
- Do you think a lot about old memories?
- Do you easily invite new people in your life, or do you stick with the old crowd?
- Do you feel very much attached to objects related with to your family?

The Second Step
Analyze Your Home: Do You Experience Forgiveness in Your Home or Office?

Acknowledge That Forgiveness is Part of Your Life

In order to receive new gifts from the Universe, we need to attract them in. But if your space is so full of old things you attracted before today, there is no space for receiving anymore. A great way to start receiving is by giving away. Giving away your old emotions and your old patterns is exactly what forgiveness is about. In your home, it is about letting go of materials connected with these old patterns and behaviors.

Obvious Signs That You Allow Forgiveness in Your Life

- Your storage place is reduced to a minimum capacity.
- You have boxes ready to give away.
- You have bags with old clothes to bring to charitable organizations.
- You have incense burning which helps to clean the air.
- You organize a networking party with all the new people you have met.
- You redecorate your home with new colors.
- You practice some space clearing techniques.
- You place bowls of sea salt water in the corners of your rooms.
- Your entrance is free of clutter.

Extra Tips

☙ The basement is the past, so if you need to store any-thing do it in your basement and not in the attic; the attic stands for the future.

☙ Do not store items at the entrance.

☙ Energetic space clearing: visualize a violet wind going through every part of your home, taking all the nega-tive energy with it and then release this wind to the outside. Do this for several days and your home will feel more open.

The Third Step
The Color of Forgiveness—Violet

When we look at the rainbow, the highest color is vio-let. Ultraviolet is the color that vibrates the fastest on our planet. The color violet will help you the most to release all those old energies as everything will be removed with it.

How can you use this color?

☙ You can place a violet item in the southeast.

☙ Wear a violet outfit when you are asking for, or giving forgiveness to some one.

☙ Place an image of, or real violets in your home.

Conclusion

When you start using the violet energy to let go of the past, you will feel much more at ease. Do the energetic space clearing each time that you feel that your home feels old and stalled.

You can even use the violet wind visualization within yourself; just see the violet wind come from your feet and move upward towards your crown taking everything with it that you wish to release. Let it go through your head and give it back to the Universe and ask it to transform it into good energy and send it back to you.

FORGIVENESS AFFIRMATIONS

I can let go of materials, emotions, and thoughts that block me.

I am ready to elevate my inner Chi.

I create space for good fortune to enter my life.

I forgive myself for my old behaviors and patterns that caused harm in my life and to others.

I ask forgiveness from others for what I caused them.

I forgive others that caused harm to me.

Chapter 14

Do You Attract Release?

I love lavender mist or anything with the smell of lavender. It makes me feel happy and so in the moment. When
I need to release something on an emotional level, I put
essential oil of lavender in my hands and smell it and then
wave it around my body in my aura field. I always feel
relaxed after this. When I need to really deal with letting
go of papers and files, and clothes, I always spray some
lavender mist around. I even have lavender oil with me
when I travel and I need to sleep in a hotel room. You
never know what happened there and I want to release
that energy. So, I wave some lavender energy around,
especially in the corners of a room as this is where the
energy gets piled up the most.

The First Step

Analyze Your Life: Are You Feeling Released?

To create a brilliant future you need to do some release work. Every time you continue to blame yourself you are still giving in to guilt and you are stopping that brilliant future from happening. You can't keep moving forward when you're wearing a backpack full of old what if, what could, what should I have done different. You can't change this anymore, but you can shift today by letting that emotional field be what it is: a great learning experience for yourself and perhaps for others. When I teach people, they tell me I have such great stories. Well they are stories now but at that certain point they were a reality. They were experiences that I had to go through and they were not all pleasant times. I could have kept them as rocks of guilt and blame that I carried in my backpack, but instead I decided to make stories of them and use them now as gifts to others.

Questions

☞ Do you feel free of your past?

☞ Do you think a lot about a dead family member?

☞ Do you still go over the break up with your boyfriend or girlfriend?

☞ Do you still dream about that examination that you didn't pass?

☞ Are you still thinking about that other woman or man when you are intimate with your current partner?

☞ Have you turned your bad experiences into learning experiences that you can now share?

☞ When you think about a person that hurt you, do you still start to cry?

☞ Is your wall still full of pictures of what you wish to let go of?

The Second Step
Analyze Your Home: Do You Experience Release in Your Home or Office?

Acknowledge That Release is Part of Your Life

Letting go is easy when you know what is really happening. Letting go is the short version of letting God be. Release is actually about letting God take care of it. You don't have to carry this anymore in yourself or in your home. The Universe/God will take care of it from here. Once you know that is what release means, it is so easy and effortless to let go. The part in you that holds tight to all this old energy is your ego. Your personality thinks that it serves you best by holding on to things and memories. Tell your ego that you think that the Universe/God knows better. Let us give it to that Universal energy; the Universe/God has never let you down. It will always take care of it; better than you and opportunities will be created so you know exactly who to give it to or who will enjoy what you don't like anymore.

Obvious Signs That You Allow Release in Your Life

☞ You are going through the boxes you've filled with pictures and deciding which ones you wish to keep and then you put them in picture books.

☞ You help to release the old energies in your home by burning sandalwood incense.

☞ You remove burial masks and objects used in rituals from your home.

☞ You replace pictures of your former partner with something more general.

☞ You hang more current pictures of your children and grandchildren. Don't hang images anymore of their baby years if they are twenty or more. It is embarrassing when they visit you.

☞ You have removed anything that connects you with a bad experience and relationship so you can let go of it completely.

☞ You have returned books, DVDs, CDs, and clothes to persons that you are no longer associated with.

☞ When a person passes away, you take the time to release their belongings, but after six months you really start taking care of it.

Extra Tips

☞ Invite some friends over and have a release party. It is more fun with others and you will be more motivated to remove things.

☞ Read the letters one more time, listen to the music one more time, put on that dress one more time, and then bless it for the time you had it in your life and let it go.

The Third Step
The Color of Release—Lilac

Lilac is the color of lavender. Lavender was used by our grandmothers.

They placed a little bag with dried lavender flowers in our closets. The smell of lavender helps us to be in the moment and no longer feel stuck in the past.

Opening your closets will give you a great feeling to start with.

How can you use this color?

- You can buy some of these little grandmother bags and put them in your closets.
- When you have a hard time letting go of people and memories, wear lilac outfits.
- Spread lavender mist in your living room, it will help you to enjoy the day.

Conclusion

Your home is a reflection of your life. When you have built up a lot of shame in yourself, you will have also attracted that you are ashamed of your home.

You will have created so much chaos that you don't dare invite anyone over. When you have built up a lot of guilt, you will have piles of old books and magazines and papers or anything else. You feel guilty letting go of something because you never know when you can use it one day.

RELEASE AFFIRMATIONS

I have a positive outlook and focus on my goals.

I release here and now everything
that I no longer need in my life.

I choose to be a winner and no longer a loser.

I accept old relationships
as great learning experiences.

I allow myself to enjoy the reality
I have created so far.

I open my heart to release
old pain, blame, and guilt.

Chapter 15

~~~~~~

Do You
Attract Clarity?

I had a client that told me that he wanted success in his business. One of the ideas that I shared with him was that you can put an image up of a boat sailing towards you with wealth and success on board. He said he had that image hanging exactly across from the entrance door of the office. That seemed good but I asked him to be very sure because the Universe watches all the details. When he looked closer he saw that the sailboat was sailing in a river and at the end of the river was a waterfall. That is exactly how things were as the opportunities came in but they all eventually went downhill. My Feng Shui Masters told me another story. Six weeks before he left her, a woman received a painting from her lover of a man on a boat and a lady on the beach. She wanted to keep the painting as she believed that the man would then come back. But if you looked at the details of the image, the man was sailing away from the beach and not towards the beach. The intention of the lover was already visible in the painting and as long as she left the painting hung there any man would sail away from her.

The First Step
Analyze Your Life: Are You Feeling Clear?

The Universe is like a large shop; you can ask for anything. If you would walk in to a shop and ask for a dress, the shop owner will tell you to look around. After you have looked around for a few minutes you will feel that they have nothing in the shop. That is not true; you just were not clear in your request. But, if you walk in and you ask for what you want: a dress, size twelve, casual, mid-length, cotton, in summer colors; the shop owner will direct you to the right dress area. You will not waste any time and you will be far more likely to find something that works perfectly. You will come out of the shop with a dress and you will tell your friends that they have great things in that particular shop.

The shop and the shop owner in both cases are the same. The only thing that changed is that you went in with more clarity in what you wished for. That is why some people have no results when they are working with the law of attraction. You have to be detailed when you put up your shopping list. The more details you provide the faster and more accurate the Universe will provide. I know I love shopping when I can walk in and look around because I have the time to manifest, but if I need something fast and without effort I am detailed in what I ask from the Universe. When I am detailed I will be guided by someone or something in the right way to manifest my desires.

Questions

- Do you create fast and effortless results?
- Do you have clear agreements with your family members and your friends?
- Are you placing your goals on paper in a detailed way?
- Do you do your daily prayer and visualization?
- Do you prioritize what needs to be done first?
- Do your clients know exactly what you want to be paid for your work?
- Do you direct the flow of energy towards what you wish to happen?
- Do you take care of what is not completed?

The Second Step
Analyze Your Home: Do You Experience Clarity in Your Home or Office?

Acknowledge That Clarity is Part of Your Life

The Universe reads your home like it is you sending out the messages. So far you have put many new images out in your home. You have played with Diamond Feng Shui and it is a good time to look over everything you have placed or changed. Check to see if what you put out is what you wish for; is it detailed enough, is it what you really desire?

Obvious Signs That You Allow Clarity in Your Life

- You have indicated what business is operating here by adding a plaque or a logo.
- You have displayed images that really show what you desire.
- You display the products or images of your product.
- You clean out your aquariums, fountains, and still water features regularly.
- You have directed the flow of Chi in your hallways by hanging mirrors or paintings.
- You indicate where people need to go to with maps or signals.
- You place a plant next to the staircase so the energy is not rushing upwards if the staircase is across from the front door.
- You use lights in your garden to enhance the beauty of your home and to create more safety.
- You have hidden the spiral stair case in order to create tidiness.

Extra Tips

- Make sure your windows are clean as they represent the eyes of your home.
- Clean your mirrors as they are symbols of clarity.

The Third Step
The Color of Clarity—Aqua Blue

Have you ever been on a holiday to tropical islands where the water (Latin word is aqua) is so clear you can see the fish swimming in it? Can you imagine that the Universe can understand your messages so clear because you have given the requests so aqua clear?

How can you use this color?

- You can place an aqua blue item at the entrance, so that clarity lives in the household.
- Place an aqua blue item on your desk or wear something in that color when you need to set your goals or do brainstorming.
- Make sure you have some type of bubbling fountain in the north area of your office or living room to attract clear insights in your future.

Conclusion

Clarity is something you need to keep working with because your desires may change. Check regularly that what you did to attract your request is still up to date. I check it every few weeks. Some long term ideas will remain the same, but some short term goals can change and you need to make your shopping trip as easy as possible in the Universal shop.

CLARITY AFFIRMATIONS

I communicate more clearly in my relationships.

I have clarity in my desires.

I decide with ease what my goals are.

I know I will receive clarity on
how to attain my goals.

I allow myself to have clear intentions.

I open my heart to allow clarity
in my personal relationships.

Chapter 16

~~~~~~

Do You Attract Focus?

When I was fifteen years old I visited the Gardens of Versailles. At one point in the visit I lost my school group. I wanted to find them so I started to focus on being the group and that the group would reveal itself to me. I used a technique that I learned at school in a history class about Louis 14th. He believed that while focusing on the government, everything would be revealed to him. I was effortlessly led to my group; I walked back amongst them and they were surprised that I just showed up.

The First Step
Analyze Your Life: Are You Feeling Focused?

In order to make the law of attraction work for you, you need to focus for a while on what you wish from the Universe; by focusing you put the process to work. Everything you give attention to will manifest. Focus is a positive way of giving attention. Focusing is not an emotional form of attention, but is a mindful way of telling the Universe what you desire. It is not that you have to focus on something because otherwise perhaps it will not manifest; that is more like despair. Mindful is giving a goal attention by thinking about it, and by visualizing how it will feel if it manifests. Not in an exaggerated way but with an objective mind. You know that it will happen, with easy and effortlessness because it is the law of the Universe.

It happens always at the right time. When it doesn't happen, it means that there is something you need to learn before it can happen, or something or someone needs to be in place before it happens.

Questions

- Are you able to focus on your new projects for many hours or do you get easily distracted?
- When something distracts you and breaks your concentration can you easily get back to work?
- Do you feel you have done everything right but still there are circumstances that block you from succeeding?
- Do you feel that all your input is suddenly flushed away?
- Do you feel that in the moment you don't pay attention, disasters happen?
- Do you feel that others try to push you off track because they don't like your ideas?

The Second Step
Analyze Your Home: Do You Experience Focus in Your Home or Office?

Acknowledge That Focus is Part of Your Life

My experience is that certain aspects of a home can really create concentration problems. Sleeping and working under beams, having sharp arrows pointed at you by proud warriors in images that hang on your walls, different kinds of music, and having several doors leading into one room can all lead to a lack of focus.

Obvious Signs That You Allow Focus in Your Life

❧ Colors used in the interior decoration of your home do not clash.

❧ If you were sleeping under a beam you have covered it or now sleep in a canopy bed.

❧ If your desk sits under a beam you cover it while you are working.

❧ You keep the master bathroom door closed.

❧ You moved your bed away from the bathroom wall or you placed a mirror behind your headboard and the wall with the mirror reflecting the wall.

❧ You have hung a convex Pa Kua mirror on the outside of the door reflecting the sharp edge of your neighbor's home.

❧ You made sure that all the books on the shelves of bookcase or library are flush with the edge of the shelf. If not, this will disturb the people sitting close to it.

☙ You have removed plants with sharp points like yuccas, cactus, and palm trees.

☙ You always de-clutter your desk and workplace before you end your day.

Extra Tips

☙ When there is too much street traffic disturbing you, keep the shades down to block the view of all the cars and the lights at night.

☙ When you have your bed in front of a window, hang heavy curtains or put up a screen so the moonlight does not distract you from a good night sleep.

The Third Step
The Color of Focus—Iris Blue

The symbol of the French kings was the iris flower: The Fleur de Lis. The most well known king that used this symbol was Louis 14th. He was very focused on his goals. He proclaimed he was the government. He was definitely focused. Interestingly enough, the story is that he introduced Feng Shui to the western courts. His palace was ideal Feng Shui for his success, and for his successors. Only Louis 16th had bad luck in this palace; it was not suited for him.

How can you use this color?

☙ You can place projects you need to focus on in maps that are in this color or have the name printed on the map in this color.

☙ Place an image of a blue iris flower in the east area of your office.
☙ When you have a long day ahead in the office wear something iris blue so your focus will stay sharp.
☙ Place irises in conference rooms so any meetings will go easily and be successful.

Conclusion

Focusing is more than just concentrating. It is also creating an atmosphere around you that is like what you desire. If you wish harmony than you need to stop the heavy rock music sounds in your car. If you wish beauty then you can start with making yourself beautiful. Use anything you have to confirm what you really desire.

FOCUS AFFIRMATIONS

I improve my persistence towards my goals.

I follow through on what I focus
my attentions on.

I stay focused on what I wish to accomplish.

I correct influences that reduce my focus.

I allow myself to dream big,
and to focus on the dream.

Chapter 17

~~~~~~

Do You Attract Joy?

When I was fifteen I moved from a dull room where I had experienced a lot of pain, distress, and sadness over a ten year period to another room in the west area of the home. Western areas are connected with joy and children. On the advice of my mentor I painted the walls peach and I came to enjoy that room. It is the room that I have spent the longest period of time in up to now. I had many girl-friend slumber parties there and I laughed a lot in there. I did attract a lot of joy in that room; inside myself and with others.

The First Step
Analyze Your Life: Are You Feeling Joyful?

When you start to become aware of the law of attraction, it still takes some time to really see the results. But one of the stepping stones is to start feeling joyful and grateful about what is going to happen even if you don't see it happening yet. Joy is the wave the Universe surfs on. Somehow we know that and it is why we love comedians, comedies, and clowns. We all need a certain amount of joy to keep us surfing the wave of life. But, if you wish to excel in the law of attraction you must have access to a source of joy in yourself and be supported by a joyful home or workspace.

Questions
- Are you able to connect with your inner source of joy?
- Even when you have a down moment, can you return quickly to a joyful place?
- Do you listen to humor, watch humorous shows or theater?
- Do you recognize the bounty of your life?

The Second Step
Analyze Your Home: Do You Experience Joy in Your Home or Office?

Acknowledge That Joy is Part of Your Life
It is good Feng Shui to have order in your home but you need to also experience some joy in your home. A home is a living energy so don't make your home too serious; no temples or monasteries. If you don't laugh enough in your life, there is something wrong. You need to at least

smile and occasionally burst out into tears because you are laughing so hard.

Obvious Signs That You Allow Joy in Your Life

☞ You have summer colors in your interior decorating such as yellow, peach, orange, rose.

☞ You have colorful artwork and fabrics in your home.

☞ You have hung funny items in your family room.

☞ You have images of children playing.

☞ You have toys and not crying clown images in your family room.

☞ You have other play toys in your bedroom.

☞ You have moving objects hanging on your patio like mobiles and wind chimes.

☞ You do not have a lot of dark colors in your environment such as black and dark browns.

☞ You have crystal balls hanging at your large windows that create rainbows on your walls when the light shines through them.

Extra Tips

☞ In China they place a laughing Buddha, the one with the big belly, at the entrance to make worries go away and to open our hearts to joy. Don't forget to rub the belly often.

☞ Remember that joy is in music as well as images. Play music that makes you joyful and want to dance. Sing to your favorite music at least once a day.

The Third Step
The Color of Joy—Peach

Have you ever eaten a peach so ripe that the juice just pours over your face; does it make you frustrated or start to laugh? That is what working with the Universe is like: You can be frustrated that it is not fast enough, or you can focus on gratitude and joy imagining how you will feel when your dreams and requests manifest.

How can you use this color?

- Peach is an underused color in interior design. It is a great color to add as pillows to almost any couch. It always brings an extra sparkle and you will receive many compliments.
- Place an image of peach flowers at your entrance or real peach flowers on your dining table.
- Place something peach in the west area of your bedroom to keep a joyful relationship going with your romantic partner.

Conclusion

I recently met a wonderful woman whose second name is Joy. When I helped her in some Diamond Feng Shui consultations, I didn't have to bring in more joy. There were peach colors everywhere; even her outfit was almost entirely peach. I told her that this color stood for her name. The energy in her home was very light and joyful. Enjoy your life by adding more peach.

JOY AFFIRMATIONS

I am grateful for my past, present, and future.

I joyfully accept the gifts and the learning
experiences that I receive in my life.

I appreciate everything I see happening as
it is the perfect unfolding of the Universe.

I enjoy fun and humorous things.

I open myself to the innocent energy
of my inner child.

Chapter 18

Do You Attract Celebration?

After teaching for several years I felt that I needed to organize a party for my students. Many times, spiritual people can also be too serious. Personally, I love dancing so throwing a party and dancing till the early morning for me is an expression of the Universe. I started to hold a series of parties with no alcohol, no drugs, and no smoking. The party started in the early evening with meditation and some circle dances. I always placed orange candles or candles infused with orange energy on the table. People who wanted to come had to wear one of the twenty-four colors that I describe in this book; no little black dresses allowed. It became a trend in Europe. I can tell you that the joy we had at these parties became legendary. Still today ten years after, people tell me they were the best parties they ever attended. The music was from all continents with some good rock and roll as spice. How can we celebrate life without dance and music?

The First Step
Analyze Your Life: Are You Feeling Celebrative?

Celebration is a thing that people do when efforts are accomplished and when you know the result. But true masters of the Universal laws know that you need to celebrate every moment of your life. As you celebrate life itself, life will celebrate you. That is why it is so important to visualize the honoring and the awards before you receive them in your reality.

Questions

- ☙ Are you displaying the awards that you have received for your efforts or do you hide them?
- ☙ Do you throw parties for an important occasion or just because you love to celebrate?
- ☙ Have you ever set off fireworks or had a pillow fight just because life is great?
- ☙ Do you celebrate other people with gifts and honors?

The Second Step
Analyze Your Home: Do You Experience Celebration in Your Home or Office?

Acknowledge That Celebration is Part of Your Life.

I am sure that you have received awards in the past even if that was just in your early school years. Even letters from satisfied customers are symbols of celebration. What have you done with them? I have seen too many golden records, posters of successful movies, and images of joy and celebration in the restroom. Do you think that will support you? Remember what you do in the restroom. Make sure you give your awards a special place. A wall of fame or a hall of fame, you are worth it.

Obvious Signs That You Allow Celebration in Your Life

- You have musical instruments displayed in the east area of your family room.
- You have images of birds or real birds placed in the south are of home.
- You have placed your awards in a visible place or in a special cabinet in your office or in your living room. If you know what your personal success area is, you can place them there.
- You have a bowl of fruit on your dining room table; especially oranges.
- You have orange candles out when you have a party or even just for your own enjoyment.
- You give orange flowers to celebrate someone's success.

Extra Tips

- Make sure you celebrate daily by giving yourself compliments and high fives when you have accomplished something great.
- Create an award book where you give yourself a daily award.
- Create an award map for your children with symbols of little suns and cakes when they have done their best.

The Third Step
The Color of Celebration—Orange
In China they have many colors of celebration such as red and gold but in every home you will find bowls of oranges to celebrate joyful abundance. When I was a child my mother told me that when she was a small girl, oranges were very rare and it was only during the festival celebration of St. Nicolas that they would get one orange each. Now oranges are easy to buy, but I still think that fresh orange juice in the morning will give a morning celebration moment to your day.

How can you use this color?
- Place orange pillows in your bedroom to celebrate your romance.
- You can place a bowl with fresh oranges or mandarins on your breakfast table to celebrate every new morning.
- When you go out to celebrate, add something orange to your outfit, even if it is socks or an accessory. People will feel your celebrative mood.

Conclusion
You have so much to be grateful for, but don't let gratitude just be in your heart. Express it in all the ways you can. Don't wait for it. Immediately after reading this chapter, plan a party. Use the fact that you have been reading this book as the excuse to celebrate. Just put your music on and start moving around. My children and I dance almost

every night when I am home and just because it is a celebration to be with my children. Any music will do. Let your heart overflow with joy.

CELEBRATION AFFIRMATIONS

I celebrate myself and life first.

I celebrate my efforts and my accomplishments.

I make my life a Universal party
with balloons full of joy and abundance.

I recognize my gifts and
accept awards and celebration.

I am an honored expert in my professional field.

I am honored for my vision.

Chapter 19

Do You Attract Abundance?

When I was growing up in my country, a gold watch was given to employees when they retired. It was to recognize the completion of their job and also to give them a small gift back for the abundance they had brought to the company they had worked for all their lives. I always felt that this was so beautiful, but I didn't see myself working for one company for the rest of my life. The only company I work for know is the Universe. The great thing is that the Universe pays with golden watches whenever you feel ready for them. So one day in my early thirties, I woke up and felt ready for the golden standard. It was just before my thirty-third birthday. As presents, I received many gold jewelry items and from my family, a golden watch. The gold standard was established.

The First Step

Analyze Your Life: Are You Feeling Abundant?

Abundance for most people is seen as financial abundance. Of course in this western world, you can do more when you have a lot of money. It is definitely part of the abundance factor and you can do more good with more money. Someone told me once that money is a magnifier. When good is already in your heart, money will magnify your goodness and you will start sharing your abundance. When egoism is already in your heart, you will start acting more egoistical when you come in to a lot of money. Abundance is about feeling the unlimited source that is the Universe and accepting that you have constant access to this all-ness. It doesn't mean you will ask for more all the time but you can. It is up to you. All the aspects of Diamond Feng Shui that you have activated so far in your home can be magnified by adding the abundance factor.

Questions

- Do you accept that wealth is part of your birthright?
- Are you ready to allow infinite abundance to come in to your life?
- Do you wish to share your upcoming abundance with others?
- Do you balance your incoming and outgoing money flow?

The Second Step
Analyze Your Home: Do You Experience Abundance in Your Home or Office?

Acknowledge That Abundance is Part of Your Life

When Feng Shui came into practice, and even in the oldest texts, they already refered to how much abundance Feng Shui can create. I have experienced this with so many of my clients, who created twenty-five to one-thousand one-hundred percent more revenues within a year. It doesn't mean that money will flow in to your home, but it does mean that the opportunities to make money will. Even so, there are times when people have received unexpected money from gifts, donations, inheritances, and tax returns.

Obvious Signs That You Allow Abundance in Your Life

- You have a bubbling fountain in the southeast area of your office.
- You have added gold colors to your environment in the form of vases or candles.
- You have placed your certificates or awards in gold colored frames.
- You have some fake million or billion dollar bills on your vision board. Not just a one dollar bill; you don't want to be tipped by the Universe.
- You have placed your financial records and important papers in a beautiful cabinet.
- You have a wealth ship filled with gold and gemstones at your entrance as if it is sailing in to your home.

- You have money frogs with coins in them on the ground in the corners to capture wealth.
- You have lush plants in your living room and office.
- You have images of you and wealthy people in your personal relationship direction.

Extra Tips

- Remove all winter landscapes in your home, they show poverty energy. Summer and spring landscapes show the abundance of nature and that is what you want to attract.
- Place your piggy bank in a closet.
- Place magazines about wealth and fortune on your coffee table or next to your bed.

The Third Step
The Color of Abundance—Gold

Gold has always been the color associated with kings and queens and emperors. Achieving the gold standard, having gold medals, rushing for gold in the west, is the dream of abundance that we all have in us.

How can you use this color?

- You can place golden items at your entrance to set the gold standard when you enter.
- Find out what your Chinese animal sign is and find a golden statue of it and place it in your personal best direction.
- Wear a golden watch or gold looking jewelry to attract abundance to you.

Conclusion

I first heard about the "Midas touch" when my English vocabulary was still minimal. Instead of hearing and understanding the word "Midas," I heard the word "mightiest."; that you are touched by the mightiest touch. I am sure you have heard of the "Midas touch." Midas was a king, who with his touch turned everything to gold. You should live your life with the intention that you also have this touch. After all, as you are the Universe, you touch everything with the mightiest touch.

ABUNDANCE AFFIRMATIONS

I complete my projects with
the intention of perfection.

I allow abundance to flow in my life.

I attract abundant people as mentors.

I achieve greater results from my investments.

I open my heart to share my abundance.

Chapter 20

Do You Attract Magnificence?

I once lived in a home in low-income housing or what is sometimes called a social area. Most of the people that lived there were considered to have an average to low income. I knew that if I wanted to be the best in what I did, I needed to change something in the interior of my home. I started by buying a crystal chandelier. It was small but it was real and I hung it at my entrance. About one month later I got a Feng Shui client, the CEO of an international company. At that point, and even though I couldn't really afford it, I hired someone to clean my home. I wanted my home to look magnificent all the time. Before I needed to pay her the first time, I had four more clients as the CEO had told his friends about me. It was not long before they came to visit me and we became great friends. I opened myself to the excellent factor and the Universe brought me more excellent clients.

The First Step
Analyze Your Life: Are You Feeling Magnificent?

The origin of the word magnificent is the Latin word magnificentia; this is about creating excellence. Have you ever drank champagne and shook the bottle first? It is a great feeling but you can also do it with the magnum sized bottle of champagne and take it to the next level; take it to the top. Magnificence is the difference between great and greatest. Do you wish to be good at what you do, or do you wish to be the best at what you do. Do you wish to be a good adviser or do you wish everyone to see you as the expert and the ultimate standard of advice.

Questions

- Do you wish to be the expert in what you are good at?
- Are you appreciative of the abundance that has already come in to your life?
- Do you tithe wealth to good causes?
- Do you let your inner light shine out?

The Second Step
Analyze Your Home: Do You Experience Magnificence in Your Home or Office?

Acknowledge That Magnificence is Part of Your Life

Have you ever watched movies or documentaries about the Victorian ages in England? The house servants of that era are always shown cleaning silverware and dusting everything off. The Victorian age was one of the most magnificent cultural times for England. Abundance was visible in architecture, in arts, in fashion, and in politics. Interestingly enough a strong female was head of the government: Queen Victoria. She ran her country like she ran her estate and she wished excellence for her country; the best architecture, the best artists—and clean silverware. Your home is your estate and if you treat it that way the Universe will bring you magnificence.

Obvious Signs That You Allow Magnificence in Your Life

- You dust your home weekly.
- You shine your crystal chandeliers.
- You shine your silverware.
- You have candles in silver candle holders.
- You keep shoes, coats, and accessories hidden in a closet or wardrobe.
- You have a crystal chandelier in your entrance or in your dining room.

- **You have a mirror with a silver frame reflecting your dining room Extra Tips**
- Bring out your good china every Sunday for lunch or Saturday evening for dinner, just for you and your family.
- Dress up every day, the more you look magnificent and excellent, the more the universe will bring what you focus on.

The Third Step
The Color of Magnificence—Silver

Have you ever seen the sunlight radiate and reflect on a lake and the silver energy of the water just makes you hold your breath. A silver lake is the most astounding view. You can also experience this when the full moon shines on the ocean as you walk along the shore. That same sparkling energy is the energy you wish to have in your home and in your life.

How can you use this color?

- Place silver items in the northwest area of your living room.
- On a night out wear a silver belt or carry a silver purse.
- Place some fake silver flowers in a vase especially in the winter time.

Conclusion

Top restaurants and top hotels know how to create magnificence. Every step you take within their property is filled with magnificence from the sparkling outfits of the waiters to the little chocolates on your bed. From the silver clock they hide the food under to the sparkling chandeliers in the entry way, everything is magnifique (the French way).

MAGNIFICENCE AFFIRMATIONS

I believe in the greatness of
my talents and accomplishments.

I allow appreciation for who I am and what I do.

I feel radiant and enthusiastic.

Chapter 21

Do You Attract Harmony?

There was a lot of conflict in my home when I was a young girl. This was especially true when my older siblings came home and my parents would argue with them about life, long hair, and politics; often until the early morning. It was about 1968 to 1970; the time of rebellious teenagers who believed in a world of peace and love. Well I didn't experience that at all. They were always arguing for some reason and did so directly under my bedroom. The only thing that I could do was to leave my bedroom and sit at the top of the stairs and pray to the divine mother Mary. As I was raised Catholic, she was the saint that represented harmony for me. I visualized harmony between the shouting and yelling. I had my tree house and when they were discussing things loudly during the day that is where I went; high up in the tree overlooking everything that was happening below. Even at night, that is where I went in my mind. The background noise disappeared and I survived those years far better than my siblings.

The First Step
Analyze Your Life: Are You Feeling Harmonious?

What is harmony? It is the moment in your life that you are just simply happy for no special reason; you are just happy. Nothing spectacular is happening; you are in harmony between the heavenly and the earthly energy. It is about feeling content. Of course life has its moments of drama that are not always created by you. You are sometimes witness to the drama of others. To remain uninfluenced by it you need to focus on your own inner harmony. It would be good to have an image you can immediately go to when you experience outside stress so your inner-self can tap into that harmony moment.

Questions

- Are you able to stay peaceful in the midst of disaster or drama?
- Do you allow someone else's emotional outburst to disturb you?
- Do you learn techniques to find your inner harmony?
- Do you take some daily inner time?

The Second Step
Analyze Your Home: Do You Experience Harmony in Your Home or Office?

Acknowledge That Harmony is Part of Your Life

Have you ever sat down on a warm rock near a river at the end of a summer day? The smell of the flowers surrounds you and you feel the breeze in your hair. You have all of the five elements present; the warm rock for the earth; the river for water; the sun for fire; the flowers for wood; and the breeze for metal. That is exactly how your home has to feel when it is in perfect harmony. Harmony creates inspiration and when you are in that energy field, you have access to the information that the Universe is sending you back as a response to your requests.

Obvious Signs That You Allow Harmony in Your Life

- You have candles burning to relax the atmosphere.
- You have a bubbling fountain in the background.
- You have soft harmonious music playing in the background.
- You serve tea and cookies to your guests.
- You have removed all the images of war or conflict.
- You have soft pillows, couches, towels, and toilet paper.
- You have a sweet odor in your home.

Extra Tips

☙ Order creates harmony. Let your family know when meals are scheduled and when you are home.

☙ Try to make family time. Keep your work energy outside the family room.

The Third Step
The Color of Harmony—Magenta

This color exists of equal parts of red and blue light. Its name originated after the Battle of Magenta in Italy. When harmony came back in the area, this new color was given the name magenta. When you need to go into a space or a situation that is very emotional you can wear magenta. When people have just heard bad news, or I need to visit them in the hospital I make sure I have a gift with a magenta ribbon or a gift in this color.

How can you use this color?

☙ You can wear magenta when you need to go into an environment that is really emotional.

☙ Have a magenta candle available that you can light after a conflict in your home.

☙ Add some magenta accessories to children's outfits so they stay calm and harmonious and don't attract bullies.

Conclusion

Harmony is not something you can create in the blink of an eye. It is the result of bringing many aspects together. But you can choose to attract it when you need it quickly and that is what I do. After stress and drama has happened around me I focus again on that moment in the sun near the river and just open myself to harmony.

HARMONY AFFIRMATIONS

I increase peace and harmony in my life.

I reduce conflict, drama, and stress in my life.

I focus on inner harmony
even in the most hectic moments.

I allow harmonious thoughts
and feelings all the time.

Chapter 22

~~~~~~

Do You Attract Collaboration?

I felt very lonely for much of my youth. I knew the law of attraction but I didn't want to focus on my loneliness. Even at high school, the friends I had were those that I could only talk to about boys and fashion; I didn't attract friends that thought like me or had the same spiritual vision of the world. Lets put it this way, I was just more spiritually mature than most of my friends. I thought about the big questions of life and had many spiritual "aha" moments from an early age. I remember that I wanted to have the experience of knowing like-minded or like-souled friends. I started writing to the people I already knew and used a fuchsia colored pen that wrote with fuchsia colored ink. I hoped that I would find someone that I could have a true soul collaboration with. I became involved in a youth movement where I started to slowly connect with people who wrote poetry and were very artistic and creative. They were very much living on a higher level of consciousness. We started collaborating on creating theatre and musicals and children's events. For the first time I felt what collaboration on the same level of awareness could do in my life. I of course chose shawls and outfits in the color fuchsia to confirm the collaboration that I had just found.

The First Step
Analyze Your life: Are You Feeling Collaborative?

You are responsible for every thought, feeling or action you take. But this one hundred percent responsibility doesn't mean you can not share your workload with others. You can travel on your journey alone or you can go in group. It is so much more fun to team up with others on your journey. You can still enjoy the ride alone but together you will find a different type of enjoyment. After the movie *The Secret* came out, people spontaneously came together to watch the movie and began to implement the knowledge that was shared. The movie itself showed collaboration between teachers and that is exactly what attracted the people watching it.

Questions
- Do you open your self to find a win-win situation with others?
- Do you share your accomplishments with your team?
- Do you share your new ideas with others so they can team up with you?

❧ Are you a loner or do you connect with like-minded people?

The Second Step
Analyze Your Home: Do You Experience Collaboration in Your Home or Office?

Acknowledge That Collaboration is Part of Your Life

When people have images displayed of "alone" people they are not only showing a lack of romance but also a lack of collaboration. They show they are trying to do it by themselves. The Universe will obey this request, but you can also show the Universe in your home, how much fun it will be if you do things in team.

Obvious Signs That You Allow Collaboration in Your Life

❧ You have a family tree on display.

❧ You have a picture of the whole family that includes all the generations.

❧ You have pictures at the entrance of your business of the management team or the board of directors.

❧ You display logos of your joint venture companies, or put banners of them on your website.

❧ You display an image of you and your mentors.

❧ You have removed any images of fierce animals attacking each other.

❧ You have images on display of your associated memberships.

Extra Tips

☞ If you prefer to not display personal pictures then find and display images of team sports where collaboration creates victory, such as rowing a boat or sailing.

☞ You can also use a ceramic friendship circle to enforce the energy of working together.

The Third Step
The Color of Collaboration—Fuchsia

Fuchsia is one of the colors that were used the most in the seventies in the United States. It was used with the color orange—celebration and collaboration. The term a win-win situation is definitely connected with the hippy movement. You do something for me, brother, and I will do something for you, sister. Brotherhood and sisterhood were valued highly in that new generation. It was a taste of the Age of Aquarius that was coming.

How can you use this color?

☞ Display your team picture and place a fuchsia candle in front of it.

☞ Display fuchsia colored flowers at a team meeting.

☞ Place some fuchsia items in your car when the family is driving together for a long time.

Conclusion

I hope you collaborate with me on this book and let me know all the inspiration that this book has given you. Please email your testimonials to me at info@theverysimplelaw ofattraction.com I am very blessed that you teamed up with me to help you create more success, health, happiness, and wisdom in your life. Thank you.

COLLABORATION AFFIRMATIONS

I learn from what life is offering me.

I am open to share my workload with others.

I increase collaboration in my team and family.

I open my heart to the joy
of collaborative efforts.

Chapter 23

Do You Attract Transformation?

When I was in my late thirties I taught a large group of students in Belgium. These students were very dedicated to studying with me. I had started to travel back and forth to the United States to pursue my dream of reaching millions of people with my message that Diamond Feng Shui could create more happiness for you. I was torn between what I had created in Europe and what I was creating in the United States. One day in Nepal I visited a young lama of high rank: a Rinpoche. He was only four years old and as he placed opalescent shawls around your neck, he looked into your eyes and blessed you. After that meeting I had a powerful dream that I did not have to choose; that if I focused on the world then both continents would be part of my journey. I felt a huge sense of relief as I had felt responsible before for the ones I had helped on their journey. Now I could let go and know that every one I had helped so far was responsible for the journey that they were on. The only thing I could do was help, but I did not have to carry the responsibility of those journeys; that was for them. That gave me a new sense of freedom and gave me the opening to move to the United States.

The First Step
Analyze Your Life: Are You Feeling Transformation?

When you start to use the law of attraction by using Diamond Feng Shui, you need to keep records of your activations, cures, and results. I would suggest that you keep a transformation dairy in which you keep track of when you made a change, and when you saw the resulting changes start to take place. Most of the time changes will happen within nine days or nine weeks or nine months. You have sent a message out and the signals goes on a twentyfour hours a day constant signal and the Universe finds a way to bring the result to you. When you use Diamond Feng Shui the way you think and feel also start changing and you receive different inspirations. Sometimes the people around you start experiencing the change faster than you notice that it is happening. They will begin to tell you that you have changed and wonder what you are doing as you look more relaxed. But sometimes transformation starts with a feeling that what you have been doing so far, is not working anymore and this will cause you to make different decisions. The changes in your home will inspire you to live differently.

Questions

- ☞ Are you excited about your life and about the changes you want to create?
- ☞ Do you have a need to change many things in your life?
- ☞ Do you wish to be comfortable in your home and no longer run away from it?
- ☞ Are you happy and confident that everything will be all right?

The Second Step
Analyze Your Home: Do You Experience Transformation in Your Home or Office?

Acknowledge That Transformation is Part of Your Life

Transformation is a constant part of your life. One of the basic books that Feng Shui is based on is the Book of Changes, also called the I Ching. Life is a constant stream of changes but many people have fallen asleep in their life and have not transformed their lives at all. They are still living in the same environment, they still have the same habits, and they still visit the same pub. Transformation is about having the guts to make a difference in your life. Changing your home is a great step. Changing the pictures and the wallpaper that have been hanging there for the last thirty years is not only a visible step of change; it also changes you on the inside. Can you imagine that what you have not changed on the outside is still the same on the inside? Shifts of energy can only happen when you open your self to get in to a state of action. It is easier to shift something outside of you than shifting a pattern in your life, but when you do this your inner self will start changing too.

Obvious Signs That You Allow Transformation in Your Life

- You complete little jobs around the house that you have been avoiding.
- You spend more time with your children or friends.
- You express your feelings more by expressing yourself in artistic ways.
- You feel that people around you offer more encouragement to pursue your dreams; they help you to find the right resources.
- Your friends help you to find the ideal partner.
- Your marriage might become more romantic.
- Your cash flow improves and the return on your investments is getting better.

Extra Tips

- Do not try to be a Diamond Feng Shui perfectionist. There is no such thing as perfect Feng Shui. Wind and water always change. Energy always flows. What is perfect today may not be perfect tomorrow.
- What you wish to attract today will be different from what you wish to do tomorrow. There is no problem in this. Change your wish and change your environment and the Universe will react the same way: bring you what your wish is.

The Third Step
The Color of Transformation—Opal

The Opal is a stone that in the sunlight reflects the colors of the rainbow. It reflects the colors: blue, yellow, rose, white, green, ruby red, violet, peach, aqua, magenta, and gold. Legend has it that the opal stone can only by worn by strong women and divine mothers. Feng Shui is definitely very feminine energy but any one can use this color. It will help you to bring your creative ideas in to manifestation.

How can you use this color?

☞ Place an opal colored candle in front of a picture of someone that you need to transform your relationship with.

☞ Wear opal shawls or shirts when you have an important meeting that can transform your career.

☞ Place an opal or an opalescent item in the northwest area of your living room.

Conclusion

Transformation can only happen if you take action. The sooner you incorporate some of my tips, the faster you get the results you need to realize the life of your dreams. Try the changes for at least nine weeks and even if you do not like the changes you see right away, let the Universe unfold the changes that your environment can do for you.

TRANSFORMATION AFFIRMATIONS

I transform the way I feel in my environment.

I live a more conscious lifestyle I receive the support I need to pursue my dreams.

I change my thought patterns.

Chapter 24

Do You Attract Faith?

The color of faith is the diamond. I have chosen this vibration as my name. It was actually given to me by my master, and my husband insisted that it would bring me luck if I used it daily. When I look at how my life unfolded, then I can really tell you that by using Diamond Feng Shui I received more faith and confidence in acting faster when the Universe offered me an insight or a solution. As I changed my environment around me I felt more confident that what I wished for could become true because I already saw the visual effect outside of me; I already felt the vibration of change around me. Otherwise the law of attraction is happening inside of you and in the Universal fields, but you do not see anything change until it actually manifests. With Diamond Feng Shui you start seeing it manifest as it is already visible in your outside world. Without using this knowledge I would never had the faith to go and live in the United States. One morning I woke up and I knew I had found a home. I called my husband and told him to start packing and that we were moving in three weeks; and that is exactly what we did. Faith was strong and in my life I had already experienced the United States as images and music in my home were already filled with this vibration.

The First Step
Analyze Your Life: Are You Feeling Faith in Your Life?

In order to create results in your life with Diamond Feng Shui you do not need to believe it will happen. Feng Shui is not a religion. It respects all religions and cultures. Feng Shui is quantum physics of and for the environment. Although the results can seem magical, it is a physical science that works beyond the physical world of cause and effect. It works on the energetic level of your life. The only thing you need to have faith in is that what you placed around you is what you really want. Feeling confidence in yourself is always a plus point but if you do not know what you really wish in details, then hang something that is more neutral, more general. If you want to have peace in your family, you can hang an image of world peace. It is more general but it will send out the right message. Your family is part of the world. The more detailed and the more focused your request is the better the results and the faster those results arrive.

I feel like telling you a second story. Years ago an older lady asked me to do Diamond Feng Shui for her home. She wished for a new romance and she still wanted to have a young child, but she was almost fifty-five years of age. So, we activated joy and rose. She met her soul mate who was several years younger but had parental custody of a seven year old son. She started taking care of his son as her own. She sent me later via mail a large diamond ring. I asked her why she sent it by regular mail and she said it was because she had faith in the diamond that I was. I did reset this diamond and I wear this beautiful cut stone as a symbol of having faith in the universe and in myself at the same time.

Questions

- Are you resisting Feng Shui changes?
- Does your husband or wife or children act up if you initiate changes?
- Do you feel fear or anger when you change your environment?
- Are you confident that what you wish is what you can make your reality?

The Second Step
Analyze Your Home: Do You Experience Faith in Your Home or Office?

Acknowledge That Faith is Part of Your Life

Some people do not feel very strong and confident at the moment that they enter their office. It is hard for them to create a field of harmony where they can make a great field of manifesting. Others feel great at their work, but the moment they enter their home, they feel weak and are unable to concentrated.

It will be important to place around you images of you when you felt confident and radiant; when you experienced those feelings. You can even place around you books on self-esteem or confidence, or images of people that you admire for their faith in the Universe or God such as Mother Theresa.

Obvious Signs That You Allow Faith in Your Life

❧ You recognize great results from Feng Shui and share them with your friends.

❧ You feel that you have more patience about your self and what you wish to accomplish.

❧ You feel more grateful for what you have established so far and know that you will receive more things to be grateful for.

❧ You experience that you are practicing Feng Shui on a regular base and that you enjoy doing it.

❧ Your have overcome your resistance to change and you are looking forward to your next Feng Shui session and the joy it can bring in your life.

❧ You see the Universe giving you results and you enjoy the process of the very simple law of attraction.

Extra Tips

❧ Hanging crystal balls at your window so that the sun can shine on them and create rainbows will create a feeling that the Universe is taking care of me. Celebrate also every great result that manifests with a little bouquet of flowers, a little dinner party, a high five with your partner. The more you enjoy the results, the more great results the Universe will send you.

The Third Step
The Color of Faith—Diamond

Diamonds are forever. Ladies that wear diamonds feel more confident. When you receive a diamante ring from your boyfriend you feel more confident that you two will make it to the altar and in life with each other. Some men told me that when they offered a diamond ring, they had really decided that she was the one for them and they stayed faithful to her. A diamond is seen as the ultimate gemstone, with great power. This power of faith or confidence will encourage you to let the universe take care of you and your wishes.

How can you use this color?

➤ Place quartz crystals in the bedroom of your children if they lack faith in themselves.

➤ You can buy glass diamond forms and place them on your desk to stimulate confidence in your work or product.

➤ Place a diamond looking stone in the northwest area of your bedroom to stimulate faithfulness in your relationship.

Conclusion

Even if you feel that Feng Shui is not working immediately, keep doing the next steps in your Feng Shui plan. The diamond stone is the hardest stone to cut, and can create a lot of resistance. Ultimately, the most beautiful energy is released. Sometimes when your environment needs a lot of changes you will experience a lot of great results. Just keep moving forward with the faith that for four thousand years Chinese emperors have used this knowledge to create success in their lives. And today millions of people are opening themselves to this wisdom and experiencing great results.

Faith Affirmations

I create the new energy that I need
to manifest my intentions.

I feel confident that by changing
my environment I will change
the way I think, feel and act.

I know creative new ways will be revealed
to make my destiny come true.

I have faith that the Universe has heard
my messages and will bring the perfect
reaction and Conclusion to me.

Conclusion

In order to make the best of this book I would like you to remember the key concepts:

You have twenty-four aspects of the diamond that you can check out to see what you have been missing in manifesting your good luck. The first step is to activate what you can and create a Feng Shui life style by opening yourself to create changes in your environment.

Check regularly to see if the message you placed in your outside environment still represents your wishes for yourself. If you have changed your ideas and wishes to the Universe, just change your environment too. Keep it updated.

Keep your office and home as clean as possible. Once you start understanding that clutter creates mind clutter and emotional chaos, you will start feeling uncomfortable with the chaos created by you or by others.

Let go of all things that you do not need anymore. The universe can not bring you new energy if you do not clear out the old energy. Letting go is letting the universe work through your home and office.

Feng Shui means wind and water so make sure you have a breeze of fresh air in your home daily or at least that the air feels fresh and smells welcoming. A fountain in your room or an aquarium can bring the water element to life.

Start today. The faster you activate the faster you will create success, wisdom, joy, transformation, and many more aspects of Diamond Feng Shui.

What is next?

You can go to the website www.MarieDiamond.com to find out more information on Diamond Feng Shui home study courses and in person world wide life seminars by Marie Diamond or by one of her Diamond Team members. You can also learn how to expand on these twenty-four aspects of the Diamond and increase your inner experience by enrolling in the Diamond Feng Shui seminars. When you feel that your home is making you sick or is impossible to keep clutter free, you can explore the Diamond Dowsing home study course and in person world wide life seminars by Marie Diamond or one of her Diamond Team members.

Have a double happy day.

Create happiness inside you and around you.

Marie Diamond

9 781722 500207